T0094615

Approaching You in English

Selected Poems of

Admiel Kosman

Translated from Hebrew by

Lisa Katz with Shlomit Naim-Naor

Zephyr Press | Brookline, Mass.

Cover painting by Admiel Kosman
Book design by *typeslowly*
Printed in Michigan by Cushing Malloy, Inc.

Some of these translations have appeared in the publications of the *Jerusalem International
Poetry Festival*, in *Leviathan Quarterly, Lyric, Mississippi Review, Poetry International, Poezja,
View from the Loft, Zeek* and in the anthologies *Men's Lives* and *With an Iron Pen.*

The originals are drawn from the Hebrew volumes: *Alternative Prayerbook; 40 Love Poems;
A New Commentary; We Have Reached God; What I Can; Soft Rags; The Prince's Raiment;
After Great Fear, The Act of Poetry* and from new, unpublished poems.

Zephyr Press acknowledges with gratitude the financial support of The National
Endowment for the Arts and the Massachusetts Cultural Council.

ART WORKS.
arts.gov

massculturalcouncil.org

Zephyr Press, a non-profit arts and education 501(c)(3) organization,
publishes literary titles that foster a deeper understanding of cultures
and languages. Zephyr books are distributed to the trade in the U.S.
and Canada by Consortium Book Sales and Distribution [www.cbsd.com]
and by Small Press Distribution [www.spdbooks.org].

Cataloguing-in publication data is available from the Library of Congress.

ZEPHYR PRESS
www.zephyrpress.org

CONTENTS

Approaching *Approaching You in English*

By Lisa Katz

Beyond the table of contents of this book lie the riches of Admiel Kosman's poetry — spiritual, erotic, serious, humorous, learned and antic all at once. There are allusions to Jewish religious sources in his poems — what is termed in Israel "the Jewish bookshelf" — and some readers may be more informed about them than other poetry lovers. Nonetheless, I believe readers of these poems in English will enjoy the process of figuring out the significance of Kosman's work in all manner of areas, including a broad-ranging spiritual one, and a material world, rooted in things.

First, the poet. "Who are you?" an interviewer recently asked Kosman, a poet (nine books) and scholar (three volumes) whose life and writing have deep roots in Jewish texts.[1] "How would you define your identity?" he continued.

The conventional answer seems obvious. The poet and scholar was born to parents of Iraqi- and German-Jewish backgrounds in 1957 in Israel, where he was raised as an Orthodox Jew and educated (in art and Jewish studies), where his four children were born, and where he taught university until 2002. He has lived in Berlin since 2003, and serves as full professor at two institutions of higher learning, the secular Potsdam University, and the Abraham Geiger Reform Rabbinical seminary, where he is academic director. He is one of Israel's major poets and has been awarded numerous national prizes, including the Prime Minister's Prize and the Brenner Prize. But Kosman's remarks may come as a surprise. Often somewhat inaptly considered a "religious" poet (if that implies traditional piety), he said:

> This might sound strange to you, but actually, I see the course of my life as one of getting liberated from definitions of identity. That is, I was born, like all of us, into frameworks which defined for me who I was, into a certain language which created a whole system of identities. In my case, I grew up in a home which was Zionist and religious, with all the burden of the past, of the Holocaust — a whole history that you're burdened with. And I see

the personal line of my life not as a line of strengthening or developing these definitions but that of being liberated from them. So that inasmuch as there is a certain essence in my life, I see it as a relic of the past, which by mistake is still stuck in my program, and which I try to liberate myself from.

And his poetry reflects this. "I told the Jerusalem city watchman," for example, simultaneously reflects several traditional Jewish stories told by a Jew or Jewish Israeli, and represents a sort of liberation from this identity, because it broadens to include Palestinian history. It also eroticizes the attraction of monotheists of various stripes to the holy city, part of a long tradition of what might be termed spiritual eroticism.

The unidentified speaker in the poem is having trouble being admitted into Jerusalem. He can't prove his identity with papers, which is required of everyone in Israel, the West Bank and Gaza, but more problematic for Palestinians from the territories, who cannot enter Israel proper without them. His memory is faint, paradoxically for a Jew, who tradition says should give up a right arm if he forgets the city. Nonetheless, he's schlepping the Ten Commandments around with him and trying to get in. But these universal rules engraved in stone do not suffice:

> I told the Jerusalem city watchman that my beloved lives here.
> But I didn't have any documents. I forgot everything . . .
>
> I told the Jerusalem city watchman that my beloved lives here.
> The Jerusalem city watchman consulted, through his army-issue
> telephone,
> the guard deployed at the station outside the Gate of Water, but
> oh no! I wasn't carrying my documents!
> I had only two tablets,
> two tablets of a loving heart,
> of a loving heart, very heavy,
> made of marble.

Kosman's deep knowledge of Jewish texts infuses this poem, which contains allusions to Exodus, Isaiah, Nehemiah and the Song of Songs, as well as a manipulation of the dialogue structure of the Song of Songs. Kosman is also an expert on *midrash*, which may be thought of as short short stories that interpret Jewish sources, and about which he has written three scholarly books. The poem's narrative brings to mind numerous examples of midrash about people having difficulty entering Jerusalem, including King David, and legends about people having trouble getting out, like Rabbi Yochanan Ben-Zakkai, who decided to use a coffin. But one shouldn't see these allusions as stumbling blocks to understanding Kosman's work. Even readers of the original Hebrew poems are not likely to have had his education in Jewish texts (except, perhaps, for the Hebrew Bible). As someone who came to admire Kosman's work without any such background, I believe that his poems' other layers most often lead us toward an intuitive understanding of what we lack. (In these Google days, there is no difficulty in finding background material, if we so choose.)

One possible way into the poem comes from Michael Riffaterre, who, in *Semiotics of Poetry*, notes that poetry changes socially normative discourse. That is, poems bring language out of its original context and point us to places beyond the literal meaning of words. Poems don't necessarily make sense in a literal universe, or they might be terribly ambiguous or contain contradictory elements. To interpret them, Riffaterre posits the existence of a hypothetical idea, not necessarily explicitly formulated in the text, which he calls the matrix, which is then transformed. In this poem, the matrix might be: Jews love Jerusalem and want to go there, a statement which is part of the socially normative discourse of Zionism, which is a political movement, and Judaism, which is a religion and an ethnicity. If we read the poem as a straightforward extension of literal discourse, the poem seems to be mimetic: a Jew wants to enter Jerusalem. Ho hum. It wouldn't be much of a poem if that were all it offered, because it would be stating the obvious. The intriguing transformation is carried by the imagery of Palestinians who want to enter the city ("I wasn't carrying my documents!"). The difference between the two peoples is blurred, as there is only one speaker in the poem. Jewish claims are interwoven with Palestinian claims, or perhaps Jews are confused with Palestinians, a confusion that hints at kinship.

This poem ends, surprisingly, with an image of barbed wire, which, in an Israeli-Jewish context clearly connotes the Holocaust. What is the Holocaust doing in this poem? This heavily freighted image is in some way Jewish and Palestinian both; the Holocaust that the Jews suffered weighs on the Palestinians because it has shaped their history too. Having the poem end with an image of barbed wire also suggests that the trauma of entrapment in the Holocaust has not yet disappeared from the Israeli and Palestinian landscape. And the poem seems to foresee the construction of the concrete and wire separation wall between Israel and the West Bank, which did not exist when the poem was written at the end of 2000.

It is not only national identity that Kosman wishes to be liberated from; he'd like to be liberated from gender stereotypes too:

> Take for example a concept like "man." I don't feel like a "man." I have some phallic sides, but women have such sides too. I have instincts just like everybody else, and I don't have a problem with the definition of the animal side, but when it comes to the definitions which culture imposes on us, like Jew, Man, Israeli, I find these things very shaky.

And so, in "Kiddush," Kosman finds that his spiritual rank as the man of the house is no higher than that of a peddler taking stock of material goods like dishes and cutlery. In Kosman's poetic universe, the peddler is not disparaged. It is good to realize the spiritual in the every-day, in small gestures involving ordinary things:

> I make the blessing over the bread and cut a slice.
> Also for you my wife . . .
>
> Because your husband stands at a low stall and like a peddler
>   counts the virtues of existence
> and the praises of a reality which includes a series of things in
>   place. Because suddenly this world arrives for him
> on a white tablecloth, pure as a shroud, and in a cup and a fork
>   and a knife and a plate.

x

Shlomit Naim-Naor offers a fuller examination of the gender assumptions in "Kiddush" in her Afterword to this book, which is adapted from a longer article that she originally wrote in Hebrew. While analyzing the customary blessing of wine and bread before a meal, and the hierarchical relationship between the speaker and his wife in the poem, Naim-Naor suggests that Kosman is not only questioning the gender roles in this particular ceremony. He may be critiquing what she calls the "sanctification of gender roles" in the traditional observance of Judaism.

The interviewer goes on to ask, "don't [you] think that there is something inside of you, some kind of Jewish spark, which causes you to connect to Judaism?" And Kosman answers in a way that brings us back to the poem about entering Jerusalem, and in which the speaker merges with the Other:

> No, I don't think so. Not from the point of view of the things I'm talking about. Let's begin, perhaps, with my understanding of what a Jew is. For me, and I think this idea passes through like a thread from the Bible till [Martin] Buber, including Jesus, to be Jewish is a kind of swimming against the general current, against the desire to be more... The movement is always a swimming against the current in the sense of giving in, of not putting ourselves at the center, of seeing the Other as a Subject. Put more simply, it's a movement of humility.

> Getting to know the Other, the bridge that you build to the Other, and it doesn't matter who the Other is, is always in some way also a way to be liberated from the place where you had been before. In meeting with the Other you leave something of your identity behind, on the other side of the bridge.

Kosman is not stripping himself of his Judaism. Rather, the liberation from one limited sense of his Jewish identity allows him to interpret it differently, perhaps more generously:

> Think about it: in Judaism, already in the 1st century BCE, our sages constituted the "ketubah" (marriage contract), according

to which each husband is obligated to satisfy his wife sexually, regardless of the commandment to "be fruitful and multiply," just so she can have the joy of sex, as a religious obligation. This says to the man: Know that there is a Subject here, and moreover, know that it is your job to love her as a Subject. The tendency in Judaism is to make people aware that they live in a world of Subjects, and that only there can they meet God.

Kosman has a philosophy of relationships which is apparent in many of his poems explicitly involving men and women:

I begin with the fact that relationships take place on several levels, and it's important to distinguish between them. I would start the discussion here with three levels, like three floors in a building: the first level is the physical, sexual level, the level of the primary, animal attraction. This is the underground floor — you could call it the basement. We have to go down to this basement, even to its darkest places, in order to see where the primeval animal in us is. It's very important, for as Freud taught us, much energy, perhaps all of our energy, comes from here. This energy can be elevated and sublimated, and it can serve us later on the spiritual level, but the engine is here, at the basement.

The thing is, the more you get to know yourself and the world around you, the more you realize that actually this basement is completely crazy. You need to accept that it's completely crazy and not be ashamed of it. Most people are not prepared to know what goes on in there . . . Most of us are afraid to go down to the basement and see our dreams and fantasies, but I think it's very important to face all that, for only in that way we can start doing the work.

The next floor is that of the psychological level. When we talk about the relationship of a couple, there has to be some suitability, some kind of "click" between the two, which would give them the feeling that they have an understanding on the most basic psychological level . . . Not only the emotional one — the cultural and intellectual ones too.

The thing is that in a relationship, you can reach [the spiritual] upper floor only by going through the other first floors. A good example is the *nigun*[2] (Hebrew for tune, melody), which the Hasidim value so highly. You cannot create this wondrous thing called nigun without coming to this world in a body, without taking a material substance, whether it's a reed or hair from a horse tail, and creating a flute or a violin out of it. A relationship is a sort of a nigun, and our sexuality, our body, and our soul are the instruments by means of which we can produce this wondrous tune.

It is not surprising that one of the many love poems in this book, "Morning Prayer," starts with an admonition to remain on the material plane:

Don't take it out of the world.
Leave it in the world for me.

The poem continues with a description of the beloved's physical movements, a thumb, an eyelid and hair. Another poem, "I suckle your oral law," humorously warns in an epigraph that it is "only" an "allegory," but it may be read as an erotic paean to Jewish law, and at the same time, a sensual infant-like discovery of that law in a woman's body:

I suckle your oral law
with small sips. The sweet teaching
on your lips, religious honey,
I suckle, sentence by sentence, slowly,
slowly, just as it is.

Lest we think that a reductive sensuality is at work here, the poet suggests a concept of a non-sexist, but sexual creation of spirituality:

The blame is not with the basement, that is, with our sexuality, but with our egocentricity. The blame is with our treating the Other as an object, not seeing that he or she exists. And this state, in turn, creates feelings of guilt in us, which create, in turn, other problems of blindness to the Other. The minute a person is able to recognize the Other and to see that the tools he or she has received, including their sexuality, are intended to give a gift to the Other — at that moment they begin to create the nigun. This is a completely different kind of sexuality, for it is a sexuality that recognizes the Other and the desire of the Other. And if you can imagine a situation in which two people maintain such a dialogue in which each one sees the other, a unity grows out of it which is very rare in our world. What is characteristic of such unity is not only the absence of criticism of the body of the Other and his or her needs, including the psychological needs, but also the insight, and the position, that you serve the Other. Not God, but the Other.

The hardest thing for most of us is to treat myself as someone who's here in order to serve the small needs of my wife, whose need may be that the tablecloth be arranged this way and not that way, and that the flowers be set here and not there. What! Is this what I'm here for? I have great things to do, I have to run to the synagogue, to organize mass demonstrations, to prepare an important lecture! And that is the great mistake: you came here in order to arrange the tablecloth exactly the way she likes it and to set the flowers exactly as she likes them to be.

"Even if it looks to us completely insane?" Kosman was asked.

The thing is that the more we do these small things, and recognize the existence of the Other, the easier these things become for us, till they become even welcome. The concession that seems to the chauvinist man so humiliating, i.e. to make his wife a cup of tea, becomes a joyful thing that we suddenly have energy to do. Suddenly you start seeing that as the only place where God is.

In his poetry Kosman expresses how religious fundamentalism can blot out spirituality by denying the body. "Hardly any room for the body, my daughter," says the speaker of "Lament for the Ninth of Av":

> The soul has seized nearly everything by force.
> Hardly any room left for the body, though
> it's true, my daughter, words were etched in stone,
> but violently.

Here are those stone tablets again. Read on and you will also find a sexual encounter between a light switch and a battery (she started it); thoughts on ars poetica; the point of view of Potiphar's wife; a God who can't be found because he's fallen asleep, and is being sought by the speaker who resides in a Jewish or a Muslim holy city (some of which are the same place); a God who writes letters; and someone who needs a psychiatrist (is that someone God? Is the poem referencing the Palestinians and Jews?). And much more. This anthology contains a selection of poems from all nine of Kosman's books, from his first, published when he was only 23, to his most recent, now being prepared for publication.

Finally, there is the matter of translation, about which I will be brief. I cannot deny that Hebrew, which rhymes easily because of its relatively small word base, and which welcomes the repetition that naturally results from its smallish amount of roots and suffixes, is very unlike English. Hebrew's guttural sounds and Kosman's tendency to rhyme provides a sound experience that is different from the experience granted by his work in English translation. But I am a firm believer that the zealous preservation of sound is in fact a barrier to good translation. Kosman in English should sound like he is speaking English, because the reader of English who does not know Hebrew will find that mimicry of Kosman's original language sounds odd, and Kosman's poetry does not sound odd in the original. By the way, he wrote the last two poems in the book in English, but in Hebrew letters — that is, they are transliterations — and there is also a poem written in Hebrew which purports to address God in a foreign language. Perhaps I can steal a metaphor from Kosman's discussion of human relationships, hoping that the translations in this book "recognize the Other and the desire of the Other" and that readers will as well.

Translators' Acknowledgments

To the poet, of course, for his joyful approach to the art of poetry and his art of critical thinking and for being a — well, mensch hardly does justice to the depths of his compassion for those ignorant of what he knows; to co-translator Shlomit Naim-Naor, who added to the project a necessary measure of knowledge from her broad store, as well as the joy of shared work; to Jim Kates, for offering to read the manuscript after hearing some poems read at a conference panel, and then to publish it; to Leora Zeitlin, co-publisher, for liking the manuscript too and working with us graciously from near and far; to Amir Freimann and Naomi Teplow for generously contributing the Ynet interviews (Freimann) and their translation (Teplow, who also reviewed the manuscript at the end and corrected it); to Ohad Stadler for conscientiously typing the Hebrew poems and inserting their vowel points, and also to Nissimmi Naim-Naor for his help on this score; to Gilad Meiri, at whose talk at the Jerusalem Poetry Place, Shlomit and I met; to Amir Atzmon, writer, student of literature and waiter at The Coffee Mill in Jerusalem, who found the word "grotto" for us; and to Debby Katz and Rosie Natan, gracious owners of the Coffee Mill, where most of these translations were polished (and where the best coffee in the city may be found).

—Lisa Katz

First and foremost I would like to thank Admiel Kosman for his poetry. At pivotal points in my life his words have given me comfort. The appreciation and passion I have for Admiel's poetry connected me to Lisa Katz, whom I am grateful to have met. I have learned not only to translate, but to listen to the inner flow of words, to sense meaning, to locate irony, to swallow each word slowly, to give its taste a name. I have learned the special art of deconstructing and reconstructing which is the translation of poetry, and which is Art. The process was an intellectual delight, a spiritual experience and the beginning of a great friendship. Professor Hamutal Tzamir of Ben Gurion University showed me a new way to understand Kosman's poetry in her class "Gender and Poetry." Finally, this anthology will be published a few months after my wedding. No existing words in any possible language can accurately describe the happiness my husband Nissimmi Naim-Naor has brought to my life. *Toda.*   —Shlomit Naim-Naor

Endnotes

1. Two interviews with the poet conducted by Amir Freimann appeared in Hebrew on the Israeli Ynet website in spring and summer of 2010 and were translated into English by Naomi Teplow. The complete interviews are available on the Rotterdam Poetry International Web: http://israel.poetryinternationalweb.org.

2. The religious *nigun* is a melody, usually without formal lyrics and sung repetitively by a group. Hasidim will sing a nigun with great feeling in order to intensify their prayers and spiritual connection to God.

Approaching You in English

מה אני יכול

אֲנִי יָכוֹל לִכְתֹּב שִׁירִים מֶחוֹל מִמַּיִם וּמִבֹּץ.
כָּתַבְתִּי גַּם שִׁירִים עַל הַשֻּׁלְחָן מֵחֲתִיכוֹת קְטַנּוֹת וּפֵרוּרֵי מִלִּים.
אֲנִי יָכוֹל לִכְתֹּב שִׁירִים דּוֹפְקִים.
חָזָק. כְּמוֹ הַתְּרִיסִים. בְּכֹחַ.
שִׁירִים מִגֶּשֶׁם. גַּם שִׁירִים לַעֲנִיִּים מִפַּח.
אֲנִי יָכוֹל לִכְתֹּב לָכֶם שִׁירִים גְּדוֹלִים מְאֹד מֵחֲתִיכוֹת שֶׁל צֶמֶר גֶּפֶן וְלִשְׁלֹחַ.

אֲנִי יָכוֹל לִכְתֹּב לָכֶם שִׁירִים נָאִים מִן הַמִּרְפֶּסֶת.
עֲנָקִיִּים כְּמוֹ חֲבִילוֹת שֶׁל שַׁחַת וּגְבוֹהִים יוֹתֵר מֵעֲנָנִים.
אֲנִי יָכוֹל לִכְתֹּב לָכֶם שִׁירִים שֶׁל נוֹף מֻפְלָא כְּשֶׁאֲנִי רוֹכֵן מֵעַל צַלַּחַת
אוֹ מַבְרִישׁ כִּיּוֹר מִזְּהֲמָה בַּחוֹר שֶׁל הַמִּטְבָּח.

אִשְׁתִּי וְהַיְלָדִים הַמְצֻוָּחִים
עוֹמְדִים לְמַטָּה כְּמוֹ קִרְקָס שֶׁל פַּרְצוּפִים שְׂמֵחִים וַאֲנִי
נוֹסֵק לַמַּיִם כְּלוּלְיָן מִלִּים. הַגְּבִישִׁים רוֹתְחִים אֶצְלִי בַּפֶּה. וְנִבְלָלִים
בִּמְרַק מִלִּים סָמִיךְ. אֲנִי כּוֹתֵב כָּעֵת שִׁירִים מֵחֲתִיכוֹת תַּפּוּחַ אֲדָמָה

שִׁירִים חוֹלָנִיִּים
חַבְלָנִיִּים תּוֹלְשִׁים וּמַזִּיקִים עַל יַלְדוּתִי עַל הַבּוּשָׁה וְהָרְגָשׁוֹת
הַמִּיֻחֶדֶת אֲבָל אֲנִי יָכוֹל לִכְתֹּב לָכֶם בִּמְחִי הַיָּד כְּמוֹ אָז כְּאִלּוּ לֹא הָיָה דָּבָר

סְדָרַת שִׁירֵי קָשׁוּט. הִנֵּה, אֲנִי קָם וּמְנוֹפֵף אוֹתָם
כְּמוֹ סְרָטִים צִבְעוֹנִיִּים לִצְחוֹק הַיְלָדִים הַמְהַדְהֵד.

שִׁירִים קַלִּים. שִׁירִים קַלִּילִים.
אִם רְצוֹנְכֶם בְּכָךְ אֲנִי יָכוֹל לִכְתֹּב לָכֶם שִׁירִים לְפִי בַּקָּשַׁתְכֶם
שִׁירִים לְאַמֵּיץ שִׁירִים שֶׁל לֶכֶת וְעַצְמָה שִׁירִים נָאִים עַל הַגַּנִּים הַנִּפְלָאִים שֶׁלִּי

What I Can

I can write poems from sand, water and mud.
On the table I've written poems
made of small pieces and crumbs of words.
I can write poems that bang.
Loud. Like the shutters. With a vengeance.
Poems made of rain. And poems for the poor made of tin.
I can write very great poems for you made from bits of cotton wool
     and send them off.

I can write agreeable poems for you on the porch.
Giant as haystacks and higher than the clouds.
I can write poems for you about fabulous landscapes while I lean over a plate
or scrub a dirty sink in a corner of the kitchen.

My wife and shouting children
stand below like a circus of grinning faces and I
jump into the water, an acrobat of words. Crystals seethe in my mouth, blend
into a thick word soup. I am writing poems now made of potatoes,

sickly poems,
ones that wound and tear and do harm, about my childhood about shame
     about rare
sensitivities and I can write poems for you and brush them off as if nothing
     had ever happened then,

a series of ornamental poems. Look, I'm getting up and waving them
like colorful ribbons to the echo of children's laughter.

Light poems, light-footed poems.
If you wish I can write poems to order,
national poems   powerful striding poems   pleasant poems about my

הַנִּפְתָּחִים הַלַּיְלָה בְּעָרְמָה לִמְסִבּוֹת
הַגּוּף הָרַךְ שֶׁל תַּעֲנוּג וְחֵשֶׁק
שִׁירֵי קְדֻשָּׁה שִׁירֵי טֻמְאָה טָפוּ
שִׁירֵי תְּפִלָּה וְתַחֲנוּנִים שִׁירִים עַל אַרְבַּע
כִּבְהֶמָּה שִׁירִים שִׁירִים אַתֶּם מְמַהֲרִים אֲנִי רוֹאָה אֲנִי גּוֹמֵר אֲנִי יָכוֹל
לִרְשֹׁם לָכֶם גַּם קְצַרְצָרִים מִזֶּה תַּמְצִית וּבִמְהִירוּת עַל כַּמָּה קֻבִּיּוֹת סֻכַּר מִתְקַתְּקוֹת
וְכוֹס קָפֶה

4

magic gardens
craftily opening at night for parties
for the tender body of pleasure and desire
poems of holiness, poems of abomination *tfoo*
poems praying, pleading, poems on all fours
like beasts   poems poems poems   you are in a hurry I see I'm almost
    done I can
sketch very short ones out of this essence very quickly on several cloying
    sugar cubes
and a cup of coffee.

תפילת שחרית

אַל תִּקַּח אֶת זֶה מֵהָעוֹלָם.
תַּשְׁאִיר לִי אֶת זֶה בָּעוֹלָם.
תַּשְׁאִיר לִי בַּחַלּוֹן הַזֶּה אֶת
הַתְּנוּעָה הָעֲדִינָה הַזֹּאת שֶׁלָּהּ,
מְנִיעָה עִם אוֹר רִאשׁוֹן שֶׁל
שַׁחֲרִית בֻּהֶן אַחַת, נְעוּצָה
בַּכָּרִית. וְאֶת הַתְּנוּעָה הַמְטַפֶּסֶת אַחֲרֶיהָ,
שֶׁל הַזְּרוֹעַ, כַּף הַיָּד. תַּשְׁאִיר לִי אֶת הָעַפְעַף הַזֶּה שֶׁלָּהּ
בְּתוֹךְ הָעוֹלָם. תַּשְׁאִיר לִי אוֹתוֹ מוּסָט מְעַט בָּאוֹר
הָרַךְ, מֵאֲחוֹרֵי וִילוֹן. וְתַשְׁאִיר לִי גַם אֶת הָאַמָּה
הַזֹּאת שֶׁלָּהּ, הַנֶּאֱבֶקֶת, בְּשַׂעֲרָה אַחַת, סוֹרֶרֶת. וְאֶת
הַתְּנוּעָה הַמַּקְדִּימָה הַבָּאָה מֵאָחוֹר, לְלַוּוֹתָהּ, בִּקְצוֹת
קְמִיצָה, וְאַחֲרֶיהָ זֶרֶת. וְאֶת הַשְּׂעָרוֹת שֶׁלָּהּ,
תַּשְׁאִיר, שָׁנִים רַבּוֹת עוֹד נִתְפָּסוֹת,
מֵאָז וְעַד עַכְשָׁו, בְּסֶרֶט.
וְתַשְׁאִיר אֶת הַזָּהָב, אִם אֶפְשָׁר.
תַּשְׁאִיר אֶת קֶרֶן הַזֹּהַר הַזֹּאת,
הַנּוֹפֶלֶת כְּבָר אַלְפֵי שָׁנִים אֶל תּוֹךְ
אוֹתָהּ אַלְפִּית. בֵּין שְׁנֵי פִּלְחֵי שָׁדֶיהָ,
אַחַת וּלְתָמִיד. תַּשְׁאִיר לִי כָּכָה
אֶת הַכֹּל, יָפֶה. תַּצְמִיד,
הַכֹּל אֶל תּוֹךְ הָאוֹר.
כְּמוֹ הָעַכְשָׁו הַזֶּה שֶׁלָּהּ.
בַּבֹּקֶר הַטָּהוֹר.

6

Morning Prayer

Don't take it out of the world.
Leave it in the world for me.
Leave her gentle stirring
at the window,
set going by first
light, one thumb dug
into the pillow and the motions that follow
of her arm, the palm of her hand. Leave this eyelid of hers
in the world for me. Leave it for me slightly parted
in the soft light from behind the curtain. And leave me too that middle finger
of hers, which battles with a strand of rebellious hair. And
that amazing movement that runs from her back and accompanies her to the tips
of a ring finger, and a pinky. And please leave her hair
gathered up for so many years,
to this day, with a ribbon.
And leave the gold, if possible,
leave this ray of splendor
that has been falling thousands of years in
the same one thousandth of a second. Between the two mounds of her breasts.
Once and for all. Leave me
everything, beautiful. Fasten
everything into the light.
Like this presence of hers now.
In the pure morning.

את התורה שעל הפה שלך אני יונק

אזהרה לקורא: שיר זה יש לקרוא אך ורק כאלגוריה!

אֶת הַתּוֹרָה שֶׁעַל הַפֶּה שֶׁלָּךְ אֲנִי יוֹנֵק
בְּמִצְיָצוֹת קְטַנּוֹת. אֶת הַתּוֹרָה הַמְּתוּקָה
שֶׁעַל הַפֶּה שֶׁלָּךְ, מִדְּבַשׁ הַדָּת, אֲנִי
יוֹנֵק, מִשְׁפָּט מִשְׁפָּט, לְאַט
לְאַט, בַּהֲוָיוֹת.

אֲנִי יוֹנֵק אֶת הַתּוֹרָה הַמְּתוּקָה שֶׁעַל הַפֶּה שֶׁלָּךְ
לְאַט לְאַט, זָהִיר מְאֹד, בַּחֲשָׁשׁוֹת. אַךְ רַק מִתּוֹרָתֵךְ
שֶׁלָּךְ אִינַק, לְאַט לְאַט, בְּמִצְיָצוֹת
קְטַנּוֹת, כְּדֶרֶךְ
הַמְּתוּקִים.

אֶת הַתּוֹרָה הָעֲדִינָה שֶׁלָּךְ,
בִּדְבַר הָאֱלֹקִים, אֶת מַה
שֶׁעַל הַשַּׁד, וְעַל
הַבֹּהֶן, עַל הַיָּד,

אֶת הַתּוֹרָה, בַּמָּסוֹרָה,
אֶת הַתּוֹרָה שֶׁבַּחֻקִּים,
כְּעוֹלְלִים זַכִּים, מוּסָר
וְלֶקַח טוֹב כֻּלָּם
מִמֵּךְ יוֹנְקִים,

כִּי אַתְּ מוֹרָה וּמַדְרִיכָה, לְאַט
לְאַט, מִשַּׁד הַדָּת, תּוֹרַת אֱמֶת,
תּוֹרַת מִשְׁפָּט, וְצַו, וַהֲלָכָה,
בַּהֲוָיוֹת

וּבַחֻקִּים. וּבְגַרְגְּרֵי הָעוֹר שֶׁלָּךְ,
בַּנַּקְבּוּבִים הָעֲמֻקִים. אֲנִי, כָּזֶה

8

I suckle your oral law

Warning to the reader: this poem should be read only as an allegory!

I suckle your oral law
with small sips. The sweet teaching
on your lips, religious honey,
I suckle, sentence by sentence, slowly,
slowly, just as it is.

I suckle the sweet law on your mouth
slowly, very carefully, hesitantly. I suckle
only your teaching, like candies,
slowly, in small
sips.

Your gentle teaching
about the word of God,
on your breast, your
thumb, your hand.

The law that is handed down,
the law within laws,
like pure infants, all suckle
ethics and lessons in virtue
from you

because you are teacher and guide, slowly
from the breast of religion, the true law,
the law of trials and court orders and religious law
such as it is

and within the laws. And the beads on your skin,
the deep crevices. I am

פָּעוֹט, אֶת הַתּוֹרָה, בִּדְבַר הַשֵּׁם, אֲנִי
נוֹשֵׁם, אֲנִי תִּינוֹק חַכִּים, אֲנִי
עוֹלָל,

וְכָל דִּבְרֵי הָעוֹר וְהַבָּשָׂר
שֶׁלָּךְ,
הִנָּם הֲרֵי אִתִּי מָשָׁל,

כֵּיצַד נִתָּן לִחְיוֹת.
בָּאוֹר הַדַּק שֶׁל הַנִּמְשָׁל,
הַנָּח בְּלֵב הַהֲוָיוֹת.

such an infant, I
breathe the word of God,
I am a clever child,
a babe,

and all the words of your skin
and flesh,
are to me a fable

about how to live.
In the subtle light of the lesson
that rests at the heart of being.

אנא בטובך, אני פונה אליך באנגלית הפעם

אָנָא בְּטוּבְךָ, אֲנִי פּוֹנֶה אֵלֶיךָ בְּאַנְגְּלִית הַפַּעַם. אֲנִי אוֹמֵר
הַפַּעַם הֶלְפּ בִּמְקוֹם עֶזֶר, וְסֵיְיב בִּמְקוֹם הוֹשִׁיעַ. כִּי שָׁכַחְתִּי
אֵיךְ פּוֹתְחִים בְּתוֹךְ הַלֵּב שֶׁל הַשָּׂפָה הָעַתִּיקָה אֶת הַמִּלִּים.

אָנָא בְּטוּבְךָ, הֲלֹא תָּבִין אוֹתִי הַפַּעַם, גַּם בִּשְׂפַת הַלַּעַז הָרְצוּצָה.
אֲנִי שׁוֹבֵר בַּעֲבוּרְךָ אֶת הַמִּלִּים. פְּרוּסוֹת גְּדוֹלוֹת. לִשְׁתַּיִם.
בּוֹצֵעַ – כְּאִלּוּ סַקְרָמֶנְט-נָכְרִי – אֶת הַמִּשְׁפָּט.

הַאִם תִּשְׁמַע אוֹתִי הַפַּעַם? בַּשָּׂפָה שֶׁל הַגּוֹיִים? הַאִם תָּבִין
אוֹתִי כְּבַד-פֶּה, עִלֵּג, בְּתוֹךְ קְהַל זָרִים, עִמְקֵי שָׂפָה?

רִשְׁמִית אַתָּה יָכוֹל גַּם לְסָרֵב. אֲנִי יוֹדֵעַ. הֲרֵי אֲנִי
פּוֹנֶה אֵלֶיךָ בְּאַנְגְּלִית הַפַּעַם.
אַךְ אָנָא בְּטוּבְךָ,

הֱיֵה קָשׁוּב לַלֵּב .
גַּם אִם הַכֹּל תָּפֵל,
חֲסַר כָּל טַעַם. וְקַח נָא מִיָּדִי
אֶת הַמִּנְחָה,
הַזֹּאת, הַפַּעַם.

בְּבַקָּשָׁה מִמְּךָ,
הָבֵן,
אַל תֶּעֱלַב,

גַּם אִם בִּכְנִיסָתִי –
הָיִיתִי בְּעֵינֶיךָ מִצְטַלֵּב.

12

Approaching You in English

Please, I'm encroaching on Your generosity in English this time. I say
"help" instead of *ah-zor*, "save" instead of *ho-she-ya*. Because I've forgotten
how to unlock the words at the heart of ancient Hebrew.

Please, won't You be so kind and understand me this once
in a broken foreign tongue.
I'm breaking up the words for You. Slicing the sentence as if it were a
   communion wafer.
Large slices, for two.

Can You hear me this time? In the language of non-Jews? Can You understand
me, tongue-tied, stammering in obscure speech to a foreign audience?

Officially You may refuse. I know. I'm
approaching You in English this once.
But, please, be kind,

be attentive to the heart.
Even if it's pointless,
tasteless. Please accept an offering
from me this time.

I'm pleading with You,
please understand,
don't be offended,

even if
when I approach
I seem to You
to cross myself.

מי שזקוק לראות פסיכיאטר

מוּתָּר לְהַבִּיעַ דֵּעָה. לָמָּה אַתָּה לֹא
מוּכָן לְקַבֵּל בִּקֹּרֶת. גַּם אֲנִי הָיִיתִי שָׁם,
וַאֲנִי אוֹמֵר לְךָ שֶׁזֶּה לֹא מָה שֶׁאַתָּה חוֹשֵׁב.
אָז תֵּשֵׁב בְּשֶׁקֶט וְתִשְׁתּוֹק.

לָמָּה אַתָּה בִּכְלָל לֹא מוּכָן לְקַבֵּל בִּקֹּרֶת.
תְּגוּבָה כְּמוֹ שֶׁלְּךָ הִיא מַמָּשׁ תְּגוּבָה מְיֻתֶּרֶת.
צָרִיךְ הֲרֵי לַחֲשׁוֹב קְצָת לִפְנֵי שֶׁמְּדַבְּרִים.

אַתָּה חוֹשֵׁב שֶׁאַתָּה יוֹדֵעַ הַכֹּל.
אֲבָל, בִּפְנִים, תִּסְלַח לִי, אַתָּה
פָּשׁוּט יְצוּר אֻמְלָל,

לְדַעְתִּי אַתָּה אֲפִילוּ לֹא יוֹדֵעַ
בְּוַדָּאוּת, אֶצְלְךָ בִּפְנִים,
שֶׁאַתָּה קַיָּם, וְלָכֵן
אַתָּה לֹא מְסֻגָּל בִּכְלָל
לְקַבֵּל בִּקֹּרֶת שְׁלִילִית.

אָז תֵּדַע, שְׁמוּתָּר, כֵּן, בֶּטַח שֶׁמּוּתָּר,
לְהַבִּיעַ דֵּעָה. וְאֲפִילוּ נֶגְדְּךָ, תִּסְלַח לִי.

וְאַגַּב, בֶּאֱמֶת כְּדַאי שֶׁתֵּדַע, שֶׁמִּי
שֶׁזָּקוּק לִרְאוֹת פְּסִיכִיאָטֶר
מִבֵּין שְׁנֵינוּ,
זֶה אַתָּה.

וְלֹא אֲנִי. אָז זֶה בֶּאֱמֶת
נָכוֹן שֶׁאֲנִי מֵטִיחַ דְּבָרִים
פֹּה וְשָׁם. אָז מָה. אָז מָה שֶׁאֲנִי

אוֹמֵר לְךָ זֹאת תָּמִיד הָאֱמֶת
הַמָּרָה. אָז מָה
אִם קָשֶׁה לְךָ לִשְׁמֹעַ.

The One Who Needs a Psychiatrist

It's okay to express an opinion. Can't you
take any criticism? I've been there,
and I'm telling you it's not what you think.
So sit down and be quiet.

Can't you take any criticism
at all? The way you behave is really ridiculous.
You should think before you speak.

You're sure you know everything.
But inside, I'm sorry to say,
you're a miserable creature,

in my opinion, you don't even know
for sure, inside,
that you exist, and so
you can't take
any tough criticism at all.

You should know, it's okay, yes, really okay
to express an opinion, even if it's against you, I'm sorry to say.

By the way, you really should know,
between the two of us
the one who needs a psychiatrist
is you,

not me. It's true
that I offend you
here and there. So what,

I'm telling you the honest,
bitter truth. So what,
if it's hard for you to swallow.

אֲבָל מִפֹּה,

וְעַד לְהָגִיב תְּגוּבָה אֲלִימָה כְּמוֹ שֶׁלְּךָ,

הֲרֵי יֵשׁ מֶרְחָק שָׁמַיִם וָאָרֶץ.

מֵעֵינֶיךָ, שֶׁאֶצְלְךָ, בִּפְנִים,

בְּתוֹךְ הַדִּמְיוֹנוֹת, שָׁם אַף אֶחָד

בִּכְלָל לֹא פּוֹצֶה פֶּה. וְיֵשׁ שָׁם,

בִּפְנִים, כְּאִלּוּ דְּמָמָה.

אָז תִּסְלַח לִי אִם אֲנִי לֹא אֶעֱנֶה לְךָ עַכְשָׁו.

כִּי כְּשֶׁאַתָּה מִסְתַּכֵּל בִּי כָּכָה, כְּאִלּוּ מָה,

מָה בְּעֶצֶם אַתָּה רוֹצֶה לוֹמַר, הֲרֵי

אַתָּה מְעוֹרֵר בִּי אֵימָה.

וְתֵדַע לְךָ גַּם שֶׁעַל זֶה

אֲנִי בִּכְלָל לֹא עוֹנֶה.

וְזֶה אֲפִילוּ שֶׁאֲנִי יוֹדֵעַ יָפֶה,

שֶׁאַתָּה בֶּאֱמֶת לֹא מִתְכַּוֵּן לָזֶה.

כִּי בִּשְׁבִילִי אַתָּה הָפַכְתָּ מִזְּמַן לְיֵשׁוּת

שְׁלִילִית, וְאַתָּה כְּבָר בִּכְלָל

לֹא יֵשׁוּת אִישִׁית, כִּי אַתָּה

לְדַעְתִּי, חָסֵר בִּכְלָל קִיּוּם מַמָּשִׁי.

וְתֵדַע לְךָ, שֶׁעַם יְצוּרִים

כָּמוֹךָ, וְזֶה יָכוֹל לִהְיוֹת,

מִצִּדִּי, אֲפִילוּ בַּחֵלֶק הָרְגָשִׁי

אוֹ אוּלַי בַּחֲלוֹמוֹת

שֶׁלְּךָ, מִצִּדִּי,

תַּמְצִיא לְךָ

בַּדִּמְיוֹנוֹת

The distance from this
to your violent response
is as far as heaven from earth.

It's interesting that for you, in
your fantasies, no one
ever opens his mouth. And in
there, inside, it's like a total hush.

So excuse me, I won't talk to you now.
Because when you look at me like that

what do you really want to say, look,
you're terrifying me.

You should know
I'm not going to talk about that either.
Even though I know very well
you don't even really mean it.

To me you've been a negative
character for a long time, and not at all
human, because you don't, to my way of thinking,
exist in the real world.

You should know that creatures
like you, may find, perhaps,
as far as I'm concerned, on an emotional level

or maybe in your
dreams, for all I care
you may find
in fantasies

גַּמָּדִים קְטַנִּים אוֹ טְרוֹלִים,
תַּאֲמִין לִי, מִצִּדִּי,
סְתָם יְצוּרֵי עֲנָק,

הֲרֵי אֲנִי בִּכְלָל לֹא מִתְוַכֵּחַ אִתְּךָ,
אִם אַתָּה לֹא שָׂם לֵב. כִּי, בִּשְׁבִילִי, זֶה
עֶלְבּוֹן לָאִינְטֶלִגֶנְצְיָה. חַד וְחָלָק.

וְאַגַּב, אֲנִי חַיָּב לְהוֹסִיף, וְזֶה
בֶּאֱמֶת לְטוֹבָתְךָ, שֶׁמִּי שֶׁזָּקוּק
מִבֵּין שִׁנֵּינוּ, אֲבָל בִּדְחִיפוּת,
לִרְאוֹת פְּסִיכִיאָטֶר,
זֶה אַתָּה.

some gnomes or trolls,
believe me, as far as I'm concerned,
or some giants,

I'm not quarreling with you at all,
if you haven't noticed, because, to me, it's
an insult to intelligence, absolutely.

By the way, I have to add, really
for your own good, that the one,
between the two of us, who needs, urgently,
to see a psychiatrist,
is you.

קינה לתשעה באב

חו״ק (=חזן וקהל), לאומרו בניגון חרישי לאחר קריאת מגילת איכה

מְעַט מְאֹד מָקוֹם לַגּוּף, בִּתִּי.
כִּמְעַט הַכֹּל תָּפְסָה בְּכֹחַ הַנְּשָׁמָה.
מְעַט מְאֹד מָקוֹם נוֹתַר לַגּוּף, אָמְנָם
נָכוֹן, בִּתִּי. הָיָה חָרוּת.
אֲבָל בְּדֶרֶךְ אֵלִימָה.

מְעַט מְאֹד מָקוֹם לַגּוּף. כִּמְעַט הַכֹּל הָיָה כָּתוּב.
וּבַהֵיכָל, בִּפְנִים, הָיָה הַכֹּל לְבֵז. קָרוּעַ וְשָׁסוּעַ, קוֹרֵס מִכֹּבֶד הַנְּשָׁמָה, כְּשֶׁהִיא
הוֹרֶסֶת וְדוֹרֶסֶת לָהּ הַכֹּל, וּמַטִּילָה סָבִיב אֵימָה. מְעַט מְאֹד
מָקוֹם נוֹתַר לַגּוּף. רָצוּץ, בִּתִּי, שָׁבוּר, בִּתִּי. חֻרְבָּן גָּמוּר.
וְטֶרֶף לַנְּשָׁמָה.

מְעַט מְאֹד מָקוֹם לַגּוּף, בִּתִּי. הֵן עוֹד בְּגָלוֹת הַגּוּף וּבְצֵאתוֹ מִמְּקוֹמוֹ, לָנוּד,
כְּהֵלֶךְ מְגֹרָשׁ, עַל פְּנֵי הָאֲדָמָה, וּבְסוֹרוֹ, וּבְזוּעוֹ, וּבְנוּעוֹ, הֲלֹא יָדַעְנוּ,
בִּמְפֹרָשׁ, הֵן הַכֹּל הָיָה כָּתוּב: בִּתִּי, וּבַיָּמִים הָהֵם אֵין מֶלֶךְ,
וְלֹא יִהְיֶה מָקוֹם לַגּוּף.
בַּכֹּל תִּשְׁלֹט הַנְּשָׁמָה.

וְרַק עַל הָאָרוֹן, כְּשֶׁלֶּעָתִיד לָבוֹא, בְּתוֹךְ אֵימֵי הַמִּלְחָמָה, וּמַלְאֲכֵי דָרוֹם,
וּמַלְאֲכֵי צָפוֹן, וּמַלְאֲכֵי חָרוֹן, וּמַלְאֲכֵי אַשְׁמָה, יָבוֹאוּ וִיכַסּוּ אֶת דַּם הַכְּאֵב
הַזֶּה בִּזְהַב-פָּרֹכֶת-הַגְּלִימָה – רַק אָז תָּבוֹא בַּלֵּב טָעוּת הַהַכָּרָה-הָאֵימָה:
הַכֹּל הָיָה חָרוּת. אֲבָל בְּדֶרֶךְ אֵלִימָה.

20

Lament for the Ninth of Av

For cantor and congregants:
To be sung softly after reading the Book of Lamentations

Hardly any room for the body, my daughter.
The soul has seized nearly everything by force.
Hardly any room left for the body, though
it's true, my daughter, words were etched in stone,
but violently.

Hardly any room for the body. Nearly everything was written.
And all is turned to plunder inside the temple.
The body, torn and split, crumbles from the weight of the soul
trampling and destroying, spreading fear all around. Hardly any
room left for the body. Crushed, my daughter, broken, my daughter.
      Totally destroyed.
And prey for the soul.

Hardly any room for the body, my daughter, in exile
or when it leaves its place to wander, like a deportee
coming and going on the face of the earth, inching along, moving along.
Didn't we know exactly, everything was written,
my daughter. *In those days there was no king,*
and there won't be room for the body.
The soul will control everything.

Southern angels, northern ones, angels of rage and angels of guilt,
will shroud the blood with a golden ark curtain,
shroud the coffin, sure to arrive in the horrors of war.
And then the heart will know its mistake,
terribly aware:
everything was etched in stone, but violently.

כְּשֶׁיִּרְצְחוּ אוֹתִי הַמְחַבְּלִים בַּחַלּוֹנִי

כְּשֶׁיִּרְצְחוּ אוֹתִי הַמְחַבְּלִים, בְּחַלּוֹנִי, עַל רֶקַע לְאֻמָּנִי, אֲנִי אָבִין אֶת מַה שֶּׁלֹּא הֵבַנְתִּי מִדִּבְרֵי הַמְּדִינָאִים,
כְּשֶׁהָיִיתִי חַי, נוֹשֵׁם, וּמְהַלֵּךְ אִתְּכֶם, אָדָם פָּשׁוּט, אֶחָד, סְתָמִי, מִן הַשּׁוּרָה.
כְּשֶׁיִּרְצְחוּ אוֹתִי עַל רֶקַע הַדְּגָלִים, הַקִּשּׁוּטִים, זֵרֵי פְּרָחִים וְעַמּוּדֵי הַתַּפְאוּרָה, יָנוּעוּ הַלְּאֻמִּים, יָמִין
וּשְׂמֹאל, בַּמְּהוּמָה, רָאשֵׁי יוּטַח פִּתְאֹם לָאֶמְצַע – קוֹל-הָרֶצַח יַעֲבֹר – כְּמוֹ כָּרוֹז, קוֹרֵא-לַכֹּל, בְּעִיר הַנֶּצַח,
קוֹרֵא מִשָּׁם בְּקוֹל גָּדוֹל, קוֹרֵא, קוֹרֵא, כְּתַרְנְגוֹל, וּפִיו פּוֹנֶה אֶל תְּהוֹם הַנִּשְׁיָּה: אֲנִי הֲרֵי הוּא הַמְפֻזָּר,
וְאֵיבָרַי דְּבוּקִים עַל כָּל הַשֶּׁטַח,
הַאִם אַתֶּם מוֹצְאִים אוֹתִי? אֶת הַשָּׁלֵם, אֶת סַךְ כָּל הַגּוּיָה?
הָא ! ! הִנֵּה, הַמְחַבְּלִים עוֹמְדִים אֶצְלִי, בְּחַלּוֹנִי – וַהֲלֹא אֲנִי בְּסַךְ הַכֹּל אָדָם אֶחָד, סְתָמִי, אֶפֶר, אֶזְרָח
עָנִי, מִן הַשּׁוּרָה ! – אַךְ בִּידָם הַסַּכִּינִים, הַכִּידוֹנִים, וְהַצְּבָתוֹת, וּמַכְשִׁירֵי עִקּוּם-וַעֲקִירָה – אוֹתָם
הַמְכֻוָּנִים אֵלַי מִן הַיָּמִין כְּדֵי לְנַקֵּב בִּי חוֹר-פְּנִימִי, וּמִן הַשְּׂמֹאל כְּדֵי לַעֲקֹר אֶת עוֹלָמִי – וּבְלִבָּם, הֲלֹא
שְׁנוּיָה, אוֹתָהּ תּוֹרָה:
חָכְמַת-הַסַּכִּינִים –
אַךְ אָז יָבוֹא בִּי פֶּתַע, הוֹ חֲזִיז וָרַעַם !
אָז יָבוֹא בִּי פֶּתַע דְּבַר-הַהַכָּרָה –
מַמָּשׁ כְּרֶגַע, פֶּסַע דַּק, לִפְנֵי שֶׁיְּנַתְּחוּ אוֹתִי בְּזַעֲמָם,
לַהֲמוֹנִי בְּתָרִים קְטַנִּים, כְּמוֹ אֵילוֹ שֶׁל אַבְרָהָם
(אֲשֶׁר נִתְפַּס לְבַד, עַל יַד הָעֵץ, בַּעֲקֵדַת-יִצְחָק :)
– הֲרֵי עַתָּה – כְּשֶׁנִּסְתַּיְּמָה לָהּ בְּשָׁעָה בְּרוּכָה אוֹתָהּ מְלָאכָה – הֵם יִשְׁלְחוּ מִמֶּנִּי חֲתִיכָה אַחַת קְטַנָּה,
קַרְטוֹב, אֶמְצַע-דֻּגְמָה – פִּסָּה אוֹ נֵתַח, מִיָּד אַחֲרֵי סִיּוּם פָּרָשַׁת הָרֶצַח, אֶפְשָׁר, אוּלַי, אֲפִלּוּ בִּשְׁלִיחוּת-
הַטּוֹב-לְטַעֲמָהּ,
פְּרוּר אֶחָד וְדַי,
כַּזַּיִת-לִבְרָכָה –
לָתֵת אוֹתִי בְּאוֹת שֶׁל דָּם, בְּאוֹת-נִצְחִי-שֶׁל-דָּם, שֶׁל דַּם-תָּמִיד, שֶׁל דַּם-תָּמִיד-שֶׁלִּי-מִכְּתָמָם, עַל הַמַּשְׁקוֹף
וְהַמְּזוּזוֹת, עַל כָּל פִּתְחֵי הַמִּבְצָרִים, מֵעַל צְרִיחֵי הַמְּצוּדוֹת, עַל כָּל חוֹמוֹת הַמַּמְלָכָה –

When the terrorists murder me at my window

When the terrorists murder me at my window for nationalist reasons,
 I'll understand what I didn't from the statesmen's words,
when I lived, breathed and walked among you, a simple man, an ordinary guy.
When they murder me against a background of flags, bunting, wreathes
 of flowers and stage pillars, the nations will range, right
and left, rioting, my head suddenly flung toward the center — murder's
 voice will pass by like a proclamation, a call to everyone in the eternal city,
calling out loudly like a rooster, its mouth toward oblivion: it's me who is
 scattered,
my organs stuck all over the place.
Can you find me? My whole body, the entire corpse.
Ha, the terrorists are here at my place, at my window, and after all I'm only
 one person, ordinary,
gray, a poor citizen, a regular guy — they hold the knives, bayonets, pliers,
 tools to twist and
wrench, the same ones aimed at me from the right to pierce deep holes,
 and from the left to uproot my world, and in their hearts, isn't it
 learned by heart,
the same Law —
Knife Wisdom —
And then suddenly it will come to me, oh, like thunder!
a glimmer of understanding —
just for one second, one tiny step, before they cut me up in their rage
into millions of chunks, like Abraham's ram
(caught alone, near a tree, in the Binding of Isaac).
Just now — when the work is done, at that blessed hour, they will remove
 one small piece of me,
a pinch, a sample, a strip or chunk, right after the murder business, it will
 be possible, perhaps, on a tasting-mission,
just one crumb and that's it,
olive size for a blessing —
to turn me into a sign of blood, an eternal sign for blood, blood sacrifice forever,
 my blood eternally staining the doorways and the doorframes, the *mezuzahs*,

*

— הֲרֵי אֶהְיֶה עַתָּה כְּנֵר, אֶהְיֶה עַתָּה כְּנֵר-נִצְחִי, אֶהְיֶה עַתָּה כְּנֵר-נִצְחִי-מֵהֵל-אוּרִי-לָעַד, בְּתוֹךְ הֵיכַל-
תָּמִיד, הֵיכַל-תָּמִיד שֶׁל תְּהִלַּת-עוֹלָם-וָשֶׁבַח, וּכְמוֹ גַּלְעֵד-קָטָן שֶׁל עֲצָמוֹת אוּטַל עַכְשָׁו, כַּחֲבִילָה עַזָּה שֶׁל
זִכָּרוֹן, לִפְנֵי כָּל שַׁעַר, דֶּלֶת, פֶּתַח,

*

— לִפְנֵי כָּל שַׁעַר, דֶּלֶת, פֶּתַח, בּוֹ תִּסְעַד, עַתָּה, אַחַר סִיּוּם פָּרָשַׁת הָרֶצַח, חֲבוּרַת הַמַּנְהִיגִים, בְּטַעַם טוֹב
וּבִרְוָחָה. הוֹ מַנְהִיגִים שֶׁלִּי! הַמַּנְהִיגִים הַיְקָרִים שֶׁלִּי, שֶׁנִּקְבְּצוּ עַתָּה לַאֲרוּחָה, עִם כָּל אַנְשֵׁי הַשֵּׁבֶט,
הַקְּרוֹבִים, מְעַט הַמֻּזְמָנִים וְקֹמֶץ דַּק שֶׁל בְּנֵי הַמִּשְׁפָּחָה.

24

all the entrances to the fortresses, above the castle turrets, all the walls of the kingdom.

*

From now on I will be like a candle, like an eternal flame, an eternal candle shining my light forever in the eternal great hall, the eternal great hall of eternal glory and praise, and like a small shrine of bones I'll be hefted now, like a heavy package of remembrance, before each entrance, door or gate.

*

And before each entrance, door or gate, where the gang of leaders will feast, after the murder business, in good taste and at your ease. Oh, my leaders! My dear leaders, meeting now for a meal, with all the tribe, close friends, a few invited guests, and a pinch of family.

שיר למוחמד

מוּחַמַּד, הוֹ מוּחַמַּד, הַאִם אַתָּה עוֹד עֵר?
הַחַיָּלִים יְשֵׁנִים, וְעַל הַכְּפָר הַמְכֻרְבָּל
הָרוּחַ עוֹבֵר, וַאֲנִי – שָׁלִיחַ אוֹ שׁוֹמֵר.
מַשֶּׁהוּ כָּזֶה.

אֲבָל מוּזָר: הַאִם אֲנִי שׁוֹמֵר-עִוֵּר?
צָרִיךְ שֶׁמִּישֶׁהוּ שָׁם לְמַעְלָה יָקוּם וִיבָרֵר.
אוּלַי הָיָה מֶחְדָּל.
אוּלַי הֶחְלִיפוּ תִּיק שֶׁלִּי בְּתִיק אַחֵר.

זֶה מַגְחִיךְ. הֲרֵי אֲנִי הַמְמֻנֶּה מִטַּעַם, וְלַמִּפְלָגָה
שֶׁלִּי אֲנִי שָׁלִיחַ, גַּם שׁוֹמֵר, וְגַם פָּרָשׁ, וְגַם נוֹטֵר.
צִיר נֶאֱמָן, אֶחָד וִיחִידִי, הוֹ תִּזָּהֵר, מוּחַמַּדִי, לֹא
לְגַלּוֹת לָהּ אֶת סוֹדִי.
וְשֶׁלֹּא תֵּעוֹרֵר.

מִי יוֹדֵעַ? תִּשְׁמַע,
תִּשְׁמַע אוֹתִי: אִם אַתָּה תָּקִין
לִי בְּטָעוּת מָחָר מֵתִים וִישֵׁנֵי-עָפָר
מִתּוֹךְ אַדְמַת הַכְּפָר, נוֹבֵר
בַּחוֹל שֶׁבֶּעָבָר –

הַכֹּל בִּפְנִים
יֵלֵךְ וְיִתְפּוֹרֵר.

Poem for Mohammed

Mohammed, oh Mohammed, are you still awake?
The soldiers are sleeping while the wind blows
over the curled-up village, and I am the messenger
or watchman.
Something like that.

Strange. Am I a blind watchman?
Someone up there needs to check.
Perhaps there's been an oversight.
Perhaps my file's been switched
with someone else's?

Ridiculous. After all I've been duly appointed, and I am a representative
of my party and also a guard, a soldier on horseback, a policeman,
a faithful envoy, the one and only, oh watch out, my Mohammed,
don't tell the party my secret.
And don't wake anyone up.

Who knows? Listen,
listen to me:
if tomorrow by mistake because of me, you awaken
those dead-and-buried in the village land,
digging up yesterday's sands,

everything inside
will crumble.

משהו מכאיב

מַשֶּׁהוּ מַכְאִיב לִי כָּאן, בַּצַּד, אַתָּה רוֹאֶה, קוֹנִי?
מַשֶּׁהוּ תָּפַח לִי, וְיָצָא לִי, וּבָלַט
לַחוּץ, מִתּוֹךְ הַהִרְהוּרִים, כְּמוֹ אֶצְבַּע
שֶׁנִּקְעָה, נַפְשִׁי הִצְמִיחָה
קֶרֶן אֲרֻכָּה שֶׁל יִסּוּרִים.

מַשֶּׁהוּ מַכְאִיב לִי כָּאן, בַּצַּד, אַתָּה רוֹאֶה, קוֹנִי?
הַבְּדִידוּת הִצְמִיחָה לִי זָוִית, בְּלִיטָה חַדָּה, עֲוִית,
כְּמוֹ נָחָשׁ-כַּפְתּוֹר אָרֹךְ, צוֹמַחַת וְיוֹצֵאת לִי
מִן הַגַּב אֶל פַּס-הָאוֹר, וּמִתְפַּתֶּלֶת עַל הַחֵיק
כְּמוֹ זָנָב שֶׁיֵּשׁ לִכְרֹת, מַהֵר, קוֹנִי, עַכְשָׁו,
כָּעֵת. לִגְזֹם וּלְסַלֵּק.

מַשֶּׁהוּ מַכְאִיב לִי כָּאן, בַּצַּד, אַתָּה רוֹאֶה, קוֹנִי?
הַבֶּגֶד לֹא מַסְתִּיר אֶת זֶה. וְהַתְּנוּעוֹת הַמְגֻשָּׁמוֹת שֶׁלִּי
רַק מוֹסִיפוֹת גֹּחוּךְ. מַשֶּׁהוּ מַכְאִיב לִי. בָּרְחוֹבוֹת
בַּחוּץ הַחוֹגְגִים יוֹצְאִים בְּרִקּוּדִים וּבְשַׂדּוֹת אָבִיב
נִפְלָא. פְּרָחִים. נָשִׁים. מַשֶּׁהוּ מַכְאִיב לִי כָּאן, בַּצַּד,
קוֹנִי, הַאִם אֵינְךָ מַקְשִׁיב?

Something hurts

Something hurts me here, on the side, do You see, my Lord?
Something swelling sticks out, juts
out of contemplation, like a broken
finger, my soul grows
a long horn of misery.

Something hurts me here, on the side, do You see, my Lord?
Loneliness spawns an angle, a sharp protrusion, a spasm
like a long button-snake grows and emerges
from my back toward the streak of light, and curls on my chest
like a tail that must be cut off, hurry, my Lord,
now. Trim it off and throw it away.

Something hurts me here, on the side, do You see, my Lord?
Clothing cannot conceal it. My clumsy movements
only make it more ridiculous. Something hurts. In the streets
revelers dance and in the fields,
wondrous spring. Flowers. Women. Something hurts me here, on the side,
my Lord, aren't you listening?

אמרתי לשומר העיר ירושלים שכאן גרה אהובתי

אָמַרְתִּי לְשׁוֹמֵר הָעִיר יְרוּשָׁלַיִם שֶׁכָּאן גָּרָה אֲהוּבָתִי.
אֲבָל לֹא הָיוּ לִי תְּעוּדוֹת. שָׁכַחְתִּי הַכֹּל, אֶת שְׁמִי וּמְקוֹם בֵּיתִי,
וְשֵׁם אַרְצִי הַהֲרָרִית, וּמְקוֹם עִירִי הָרְחוֹקָה
וְהַנָּכְרִית, בִּצְעִידָתִי, הָאֲרֻכָּה
וְהָרַגְלִית – מִשָּׁם וְעַד פִּתְחֵי הָעִיר בָּהּ נָמָה לָהּ
עַתָּה,
בְּשַׁלְוָתָהּ,
אֲהוּבָתִי !

אָמַרְתִּי לְשׁוֹמֵר הָעִיר יְרוּשָׁלַיִם שֶׁכָּאן גָּרָה אֲהוּבָתִי.
שׁוֹמֵר הָעִיר יְרוּשָׁלַיִם פָּנָה בַּפְנִימִי לְשׁוֹמֵר הָעִיר
הַחִיצוֹנִי, זֶה הַמֻּצָּב לוֹ בְּעֶמְדַת שַׁעַר הַמַּיִם, אֲבָל –
אֲבוֹי ! לֹא נָשָׂאתִי עִמִּי תְּעוּדוֹת !
הָיוּ עָלַי רַק שְׁנֵי לוּחוֹת !
רַק שְׁנֵי לוּחוֹת שֶׁל לֵב אוֹהֵב.
שֶׁל לֵב אוֹהֵב, כָּבֵד מְאֹד,
מַשִּׁישׁ.

מָה אֲנִי יָכוֹל לַעֲשׂוֹת ! ? !
אִמְרוּ נָא לִי, שׁוֹמְרִים שֶׁלִּי,
שׁוֹמְרִים טוֹבִים, נוֹטְרִים, וּמְגִנֵּי הָעִיר,
שׁוֹמְרֵי גַּרְעִין-הַטּוֹב-וְהַיָּקָר –
כִּי לֹא הָיָה לִי שׁוּם תַּצְלוּם בַּכִּיס,
אוֹ תְּעוּדוֹת-נְיָר !

רַק תְּעוּדוֹת בַּרְזֶל,
וּתְעוּדוֹת מֵאֶבֶן,
וּתְעוּדוֹת-שָׁנִים, מִתְפּוֹרְרוֹת, שֶׁל גִּיר.

I told the Jerusalem city watchman that my beloved lives here

I told the Jerusalem city watchman that my beloved lives here.
But I didn't have any documents. I forgot everything,
my name and my place of origin,
the name of my hilly country
and the site of my distant and foreign town
from which I marched a long way by foot
to the edge of the city
where she rests
in tranquility,
my beloved!

I told the Jerusalem city watchman that my beloved lives here.
The Jerusalem city watchman consulted, through his army-issue telephone,
the guard deployed at the station outside the Gate of Water, but
oh no! I wasn't carrying my documents!
I had only two tablets,
two tablets of a loving heart,
of a loving heart, very heavy,
made of marble.

What am I to do?
Please tell me, my watchmen,
good watchmen, guards, defenders of the city,
defenders of the precious core.
I didn't have a photo in my pocket,
or paper documents!

Only iron certificates,
certificates in stone,
crumbling historical chalk documents.

שׁוֹמְרִים! שׁוֹמְרֵי הַכֹּתֶל וְהַקִּיר!
שׁוֹמְרִים שֶׁלִּי! שׁוֹמְרֵי הָעִיר,
בָּהּ נָמָה לָהּ עַתָּה,
בְּמִטָּתָהּ,
בְּשַׁלְוָתָהּ,
אֲהוּבָתִי!

אַתֶּם, אַתֶּם — שׁוֹמְרִים־דְּבֵקִים־בַּמְּשִׂימָה,
וּמֻצָּבִים עַתָּה בַּחֲרַכִּים, עַל קִיר־חוֹמָה —
שִׁמְעוּ, שִׁמְעוּ,
אֲנִי קוֹרֵא לְעֶזְרַתְכֶם
מִפַּאֲתֵי הָעִיר:

הַאִם תּוּכְלוּ, בְּבַקָּשָׁה,
רַק לְהָעִיר
אוֹתָהּ — לוּ לְדַקָּה,
אֶת יָפָתִי —

אֶת יָפָתִי
הַנָּמָה לָהּ
עַתָּה,
בְּשַׁלְוָתָהּ,

בְּתוֹךְ עִירִי, שֶׁלִּי,
עַל מִטָּתָהּ??

אָנָּא מִכֶּם, שׁוֹמְרֵי הָעִיר יְרוּשָׁלַיִם!
קִרְאוּ לָהּ! הָעִירוּהָ! בָּאֶלְחוּטִי אוֹ בַּנַּיָּד!
שׁוֹמְרֵי הָעִיר, הַגִּבּוֹרִים וּבְנֵי הַחַיִל!
בְּבַקָּשָׁה, בְּבַקָּשָׁה קִרְאוּ לָהּ!
שֶׁתָּבוֹא אֵלַי מִיָּד!

אוּלַי הִיא מוּכָנָה??
אוּלַי הִיא כְּבָר נוֹטֶפֶת־מוֹר
וּלְבוֹנָה??

32

Watchmen! Guards of the Western Wall!
My watchmen! Guards of the city
where she rests now
in her bed
in tranquility
my beloved!

You, you — watchmen devoted to your task,
deployed now at the portals in the walls.
Listen, listen,
I'm calling on you for help
from the outskirts of the city.

Could you please
just wake her
up — just for a minute —
my beauty —

my beauty
sleeping now
in tranquility
inside my city, mine,
in her bed??

Please, one of you guards of the city of Jerusalem,
call to her! Wake her up! With a cordless or a mobile phone!
Watchers of the city, heroes and soldiers!
Please, please, call to her!
To come to me right now!

Perhaps she's ready??
Perhaps she's already dripping with frankincense
and myrrh??

וַעֲטוּפָה —
בַּעֲבוּרִי לְבַד —
בִּכְתֹנֶת-
לַיְל ? ?

אוּלַי אֶרְאֶה
אוֹתָהּ,
עַתָּה ?

אוּלַי תָּרִים אֵלַי
אֶת מַבָּטָהּ —

מֵאֲחוֹרֵי הַתַּיִל ? ?

And wrapped —
for me alone —
in a night-
gown??

Perhaps I'll see
her,
now?
Perhaps she'll lift her gaze
to me —

from behind the barbed wire??

פסוקים אחרונים: השלמה לספר דברים

עֲזֹב, בְּחַיֶּיךָ,
אַל תַּעֲשֶׂה מִזֶּה עִנְיָן,
כְּתֹב שֶׁנּוֹלַדְנוּ, הָיִינוּ, טָבַעְנוּ בַּיָּם.
דַּי בָּזֶה. קַצֵּר, בְּטוּבְךָ, פְּסוּקִים
אַחֲרוֹנִים, וּרְמֹז רַק שֶׁרַע כָּאן,
וְאֵין אַהֲבָה, וּבַמִּדְבָּר, כָּל הַדֶּרֶךְ, זְקֵנִים
וְרוֹגְנִים, וּמֵתִים עוֹד לִפְנֵי כֵן,
מַסָּה וּמְרִיבָה,

וְתִינוֹק הַמּוֹלֶדֶת, אֵיבָה, בֶּן יוֹמוֹ, וְתִינוֹק
הַמּוֹלֶדֶת, עָרְפָּה, הִיא אִמּוֹ, וְתִינוֹק
הַמּוֹלֶדֶת, דִּיסָה, וְחָלָב,
וְגוֹמֵעַ, תּוֹסֶפֶת,
מֵתִים וְרָעָב.

וּכְתֹב בְּקִצּוּר עַל הַהֶרֶג, הַדָּם,
וּרְמֹז בִּקְצָרָה לַמּוֹלֶדֶת, לְעָם,
וְקַצֵּר, בְּטוּבְךָ (הֲרֵי אֵין כָּאן
עִנְיָן), וְתַזְכִּיר לַקּוֹרֵא
שֶׁטָּבַעְנוּ בַּיָּם.

36

Verses to Be Added to the End of Deuteronomy

Are you kidding, let it be,
just write that we were born, we were here,
and we drowned in the sea.
Enough. Keep the final verses short,
if you please, just hint that it's bad here,
no love in the desert, the old people grumbling,
even dying all the way here,
adversity and *contention*.

And the day-old baby of the homeland — hatred —
the baby of the homeland, and its mother — longing,
and the baby of the homeland,
swallowing oatmeal and milk, some more,
dying and hunger.

Write concisely about killing and blood,
just hint at a people and a homeland,
keep it short, if you please (let it be),
and remind the reader
that we drowned in the sea.

אֲנִי מַעֲמִיד דְּבָרִים בְּרוּרִים נָמוּךְ עַל גֹּבַהּ הַשֻּׁלְחָן.
אֵינֶנִּי מַטְעֶה, אֵינֶנִּי מַסְתִּיר, מִן הַגֹּבַהּ הַזֶּה הָרָחוּף עֲבוּרִי
אֵינֶנּוּ מוֹסִיף דָּבָר.
וְכָךְ יֵשׁ לִרְאוֹת אֶת סִדְרַת הַדְּבָרִים הַמֻּנַּחַת,
בְּמַפָּה לְבָנָה וּבְכוֹס וּבְמַזְלֵג וּבְסַכִּין וְצַלַּחַת.

אֲנִי מְבָרֵךְ עַל הַלֶּחֶם וּבוֹצֵעַ פְּרוּסָה.
גַּם עֲבוּרֵךְ אִשְׁתִּי. אֲנִי מְבָרֵךְ עַל הַיַּיִן, וְלוֹגֵם
רְבִיעִית. אֲנִי מוֹצִיא אוֹתָךְ בָּזֶה בְּבִרְכָתִי. בָּרוּךְ הַמּוֹצִיא
אֶל עוֹלָמוֹ זָכָר מוּל נְקֵבָה. וְאַתְּ, הֲלֹא תִּשְׁתִּי מִכּוֹסִי אֶת הַנּוֹזֵל
הַזֶּה, וְתֵצְאִי יְדֵי חוֹבָה.

כִּי בַּעֲלֵךְ עַל דּוּכָן נָמוּךְ עוֹמֵד וּמוֹנֶה כְּרוֹכֵל מַעֲלוֹת לַקִּיּוּם וּשְׁבָחִים
לַמְּצִיאוּת הַכּוֹלֶלֶת סִדְרַת דְּבָרִים מֻנַּחַת. כִּי בָּא הָעוֹלָם-הַזֶּה פִּתְאֹם בִּשְׁבִילוֹ
בְּמַפָּה לְבָנָה, הַצַּחָה כְּתַכְרִיךְ, וּבְכוֹס וּבְמַזְלֵג וּבְסַכִּין וְצַלַּחַת.

Kiddush

I place obvious things down low on the table top.
I'm not misleading anyone, I'm not hiding anything, from this height, for me,
hovering doesn't add anything.
And so you can see the series of things where they were placed
on the white tablecloth, cup, fork, knife, and plate.

I make the blessing over the bread and cut a slice.
Also for you my wife. I make the blessing over the wine, sip
one-fourth. I exempt you in this way in my blessing, blessed is the one who
        brings forth
male and female into the world. And you, indeed, will drink this
liquid from my cup, and be done with your obligations.

Because your husband stands at a low stall and like a peddler counts the
        virtues of existence
and the praises of a reality which includes a series of things in place.
        Because suddenly this world arrives for him
on a white tablecloth, pure as a shroud, and in a cup and a fork and a knife
        and a plate.

כשנדלקה המנורה

הַבָּטֶרְיָה אָמְרָה לַמֶּתֶג שֶׁיִּשְׁכַּב אִתָּהּ.
"כֵּן" – אָמַר הַמֶּתֶג, לַבֹּרֶג בַּתִּקְרָה,
וְהַבֹּרֶג קָרָא לַחוּט, וְהַחוּט קָרָא לַבַּרְזֶל, וְהַבַּרְזֶל, בְּגוּף
חָמוּם לוֹהֵט, בּוֹעֵר כֻּלּוֹ, בָּא לְהַצִּית אֶת הַחַשְׁמַל,

"שֶׁהַחַשְׁמַל יִשְׁכַּב !" – פָּנָה אֵלָיו בִּצְעָקָה הַמֶּתֶג
הַמְּסוֹבָב – "שֶׁהַחַשְׁמַל יִשְׁכַּב –
אִם אֵין בְּרֵרָה ! !".

וְהַחַשְׁמַל תָּפַס בָּעֲלָטָה אֶת הַנּוּרָה,
הַמְּעוֹפֶפֶת לָהּ, כְּמוֹ צִפּוֹר קְדוּמָה,
עַל הַתִּקְרָה, וְאָז, מִצְּדוּדִיתֵךְ,
בַּחֹשֶׁךְ הַנּוֹרָא,
רָאִיתִי אֵיךְ,

אֶת כָּל עָרְפֵּךְ,
לְחָיֵךְ,
מִצְחֵךְ,

פִּלְחָה הַהֶאָרָה.

When the Lamp Lit

The battery asked the light switch to sleep with her.
"Yes," said the switch to the screw in the ceiling,
and the screw called to the wire, and the wire to the metal,
and the metal, completely on fire
inside the body of a scalding heating element,
ignited the electricity.

"Let the electricity sleep with her," shouted the turned-on switch,
"Let the electricity sleep with her —
if there's no alternative."

And in the darkness the electricity caught the light bulb,
flying like an ancient bird
near the ceiling,
and then, I saw,
your profile,
in the terrible darkness,

the nape of your neck,
your cheek,
your forehead,

pierced by the light.

משורר

נָא הִשְׁתַּמְּשׁוּ בְּבַקָּשָׁה לְנִסּוּיִים
בַּגּוּף שֶׁלִּי. הָעוֹר שֶׁלִּי חָלָק.
אֲנִי עוֹשֶׂה לִי חֲטָאִים
גְּדוֹלִים מְאֹד בַּיָּד.
בַּחֶדֶר הַפְּנִימִי, אֲנִי, לְבַד,
בִּיסוֹדִיּוּת, עוֹבֵר עַל הַתַּרְיָ"ג.

בָּנִיתִי סְדוֹם קְטַנָּה,
עַל הַמִּטָּה שֶׁלִּי, לְנִסּוּיִים.
בָּנִיתִי עֲמֹרָה.
הִשְׁתַּמְּשׁוּ בִּי, נָא, בְּבַקָּשָׁה:
לִדְבַר מִצְוָה אוֹ עֲבֵרָה.
כְּלַל-יִשְׂרָאֵל !
עֲשׂוּ בִּי נִסּוּיִים !

פִּתְחוּ, נַקּוּ בִּפְנִים,
כְּמוֹ בְּדָגִים, אֶת הַמְּשֻׁבָּשׁ,
וּבְכוּ, הִתְלוֹנְנוּ מָרָה.

מִרְחוּ אוֹתִי, כְּנַעֲרָה,
טִבְלוּ אוֹתִי בִּדְבַשׁ,
וּתְלוּ אוֹתִי, מַדַּעְתִּי,
קָשׁוּר בַּחֲגוֹרָה:

כּוֹפֵר, פּוֹשֵׁעַ-יִשְׂרָאֵל,
עוֹבֵר עַל הַתּוֹרָה.

בַּחֶדֶר הַפְּנִימִי עֲדַיִן אוֹר חַלָּשׁ.
וְטוֹב מְאֹד שֶׁעַל קִבְרֵי הַצִּיבוּר רַבָּנִים שׁוּרָה.
כְּלַל-יִשְׂרָאֵל עוֹשֶׂה בִּי נִסּוּיִים כָּעֵת. בַּמִּנְהָרָה,
בִּפְנִים, מָקוֹם, וְצַוָּר, חָרָךְ צַיִּיר, נִקְרָה.

42

A Poet

Please use my body
for experiments. My skin is smooth.
I often commit great sins
with my hand. In the inner chamber, I, by myself,
methodically break all 613 *mitzvot*.

I have built a miniature Sodom,
on my bed, for experiments.
I have built Gomorrah.
Use me please:
for a good deed or an infraction.
Body of Israel!
Experiment on me!

Open me up, clean me
like a fish, of flaws,
then weep and complain bitterly.

Spread me with honey
like a young woman, dip me in it
and hang me from my thoughts
with a belt:

heretic, criminal,
breaker of religious law.

In the inner room there's still a faint light.
It's very good that the rabbis stood in line at my grave.
All the Jewish people experiment on me now. In the tunnel,
inside, a place and a rock, a tiny crevice, a grotto.

וְשָׁם, הָאִכָּרִים שֶׁבִּי, בּוֹכִים.
חוֹרְשִׁים שָׂדֶה,
שׁוֹתְלִים תַּלְמֵי שִׁירָה.

וּבִתְמוּרָה,
מִיָּד, עַל הַנָּהָר, הָאֲנָסִים-
שֶׁבִּי, בּוֹנִים לִי
שֶׁלֶד קַשׁ.

קְצִינִים שֶׁל רֵעַ, לֵיצָנֵי הַחֲבוּרָה,
מוֹתְחִים לְאַט אֶת הַשִּׁירִים,
וּמַנִּיחִים אוֹתִי.
גְּוִילִים עַל הַדַּרְגָּשׁ.

44

And there, the farmers within me cry,
plowing the field,
planting furrows of poetry.

Immediately,
in return, on paper, the rapists-
inside-me build
a skeleton of straw.

Rulers of evil, a bunch of clowns,
stretch the poems slowly,
and they put me down.
Parchment pages on the rack.

חֲלִיפַת יָמִים מֵאוֹר

(הוּעֲתַק בְּשִׁנּוּיִים קַלִּים מִנֻּסַּח מוֹדָעָה-תְּלוּיָה בַּגִּנָּה הַצִּבּוּרִית)

יֵשׁ לָנוּ אַרְבָּעָה יְלָדִים טוֹבִים
יְרוּשָׁלַיִם, שְׁזֻקוּקִים, בִּדְחִיפוּת גְּדוֹלָה,
לְגוּפִיּוֹת, לְתַחְתּוֹנִים,
לְסֵט חוּלְצוֹת וּמִכְנָסַיִם —

לַחֲלִיפוֹת מַלְבּוּשׁ, דַּקּוֹת,
שְׁקוּפוֹת מְאֹד, מֵאוֹר.

הֵם, הָאַרְבָּעָה, צְרִיכִים לָלֶכֶת. הֵם
צְרִיכִים לְבַד לָלֶכֶת
לְבֵית-סֵפֶר וְלַחֲזוֹר !

וּמִי יִקַּח אוֹתָם לְשָׁם ?
וּמִי יִפְתּוֹר לָהֶם אֶת הַחִידָה
שֶׁל הַחַיִּים ? אֶת הַפְּלִיאָה ?
אֶת הַמָּשָׁל ?

פֶּלַח הָעֶרְוָה הַמְקוֹעָר שֶׁל הָעוֹלָם
שָׁלַח אוֹתָם, אֶל הַחַיִּים, לְלֹא מַזָּל —

כְּמוֹ טִיל-קְרִיאָה עָצוּם !
אֶל הֶחָלָל ! ! !

הַמִּסְכֵּנִים ! ! יְרַחֵם הַשֵּׁם עֲלֵיהֶם,
וְיַשְׁלִיךְ לָהֶם גַּלְגַּל —

46

Ordinary Clothing Made of Light

*Copied with minor changes
from an announcement on
a message board in a public park.*

We have four fine children,
well-behaved, with an immediate need
for undershirts, underpants,
and sets of clothes —

for thin, transparent suits
made from the light.

These four must walk
alone each day
to school and back!

Who will take them?
Who will help them solve
life's riddle? Marvel?
Parable?

A concave section of the world's vagina
sent them off unlucky to life —

like giant rockets!
they were launched into space!!

Poor things!! May God have pity on them,
and toss them a lifesaver —

הֵם, הֲרֵי, צָפִים
וְנֶאֱבָקִים עַתָּה, לְבַד,
בַּמֶּרְחָבִים הָאַדִּירִים
שֶׁל הַגָּלַקְסִיָּה, מִבְּלִי
שִׁוּוּי-מִשְׁקָל!!

הֲלֹא הֵם רְטוּבִים!!
הֵם רְטוּבִים עַד הַלֵּשֶׁד!!
וְהֵם חוֹלִים!!
וְרוֹעֲדִים מִקֹּר!!

הָאַרְבָּעָה הַיְלָדִים טוֹבִים כָּל-כָּךְ יְרוּשָׁלַיִם!
אֲשֶׁר צְרִיכִים לָלֶכֶת —
לָלֶכֶת לְבֵי"ס וְלַחֲזוֹר —

וּלְאִישׁ בַּיְקוּם כָּאן לֹא אִכְפַּת!!

אָנָּא קוּם בְּבַקָּשָׁה, אֶזְרָח יָקָר,
וְהִתְגַּיֵּס לַמְּשִׂימָה נִרְגֶּשֶׁת.
וּשְׁלַח לָהֶם תְּרוּמָה צְנוּעָה
לַכְּתוֹבֶת הָרְשׁוּמָה בַּצַּד
(אִם יֵשׁ לָךְ —
אֲפִילוּ מְשׁוּמֶּשֶׁת):

חֲלִיפַת-יָמִים מֵאוֹר.

They, after all, hover alone,
struggling now,
with the vast expanses of the galaxy —
lacking a sense of balance!!

Aren't they wet!!
Soaked to the bone!!
Sick!!
And shaking in the cold!!

These four fine children!
who must go —
and walk to school and back —

No one in the cosmos cares!!

Please arise, dear citizen,
and enlist in a moving cause.
Send a modest contribution
to the address below
and if you have —
(even used)

clothing made of light.

זר פרחים לבת שלושים ושתים

אָשַׁמְתִּי וְצָעַרְתִּי וּמָרַטְתִּי בְּחָזְקָה, וּלְחִנָּם, אֲנִי מוֹדָה, אֶת
שַׁלְשְׁלוֹת הָעֲצַבִּים הָרְגִישׁוֹת שֶׁלָּךְ, וְלֹא עָלְתָה לָךְ אֲרוּכָה
מִכָּל הַדְּבוּרִים. אֲנִי רוֹאָה. אֲנִי רוֹאָה
הֵיטֵב מִכָּאן אֶת הַמַּבָּט הָרַךְ וְהַמֵּמִיס שֶׁלָּךְ. אוֹתוֹ אֲנִי
מַחֲלִיף בְּזֶה הָעֲסִיסִי שֶׁלִּי, הַמְלַכְלָךְ. עוֹלָה מִתּוֹךְ הַגְּבָעוֹלִים,
מוּלָךְ, אֲנִי הוֹלֵךְ וּמִתְנַשֵּׂא כְּפֶרֶא-עַד יָרֹק וָבָר, אִשְׁתִּי,
נִצָּב-גִּילִי בְּכַף-גִּילֵךְ שֶׁלָּךְ נִסְגָּר, כְּמוֹ עֵץ טָרִי, מַטֶּה
מָלֵא וּמְחֻבָּר. וְעַל שׁוּם כָּךְ אֲנִי
יָתֵד, בַּרְזֶל-כָּבֵד, אֲנִי קְרָסִים, אֲנִי קַרְדֹּם נִשְׁלָח.
וְשֶׁעַל-כֵּן אֲנִי גַּם אַכְזָרִי מְעַט יוֹתֵר,
וּמִנְהָגַי מֻפְקָר.

Apology

A bouquet for your 32nd birthday

It's my fault I made you sad, plucking hard at your sensitive nerve strings
— in vain, I admit — and you weren't comforted
by all the talk. I understand. I understand
very well your soft and melting glance.
I'll trade it for my sleazy, juicy one. Rising from stalks,
facing you, I grow tall like a wild evergreen —
my wife, my knife-age closes in on your palm-age —
like a new tree, a rod
swollen and connected. And because of this
I am a heavy iron, a tent pin, hook, an axe at the ready,
and because of this I'm also a little crueler
and my ways are wanton.

יֵשׁ סִימָנִים בַּבַּיִת, כָּךְ אִשְׁתִּי אוֹמֶרֶת,
סִימָנִים שֶׁל אֶצְבָּעוֹת, בַּחֲרִירֵי הַבַּיִת, בָּרִצְפּוֹת.
יֶשְׁנָהּ עֵדוּת לְנוֹכְחוּתָם.
וְאַךְ, אֲנִי תּוֹהֶה, בִּפְנֵי עַצְמִי, כֵּיצַד
אָנִיחַ לָהּ מָקוֹם, לִרְגִישׁוּתָהּ הַמְשֻׁנָּה,
הֲלֹא הָיוּ. יִהְיוּ. יֶשְׁנָם.

אוּלָם, הִיא מִתְעַקֶּשֶׁת, הָעִנְיָן הַזֶּה סִמְלִי, כְּלָלִי, אֵינֵךְ מֵבִין, כְּמוֹ בֶּגֶד,
הִיא אוֹמֶרֶת, וְהוֹפֶכֶת, לְדֻגְמָה, בְּכַף-יָדָהּ אֶת הַפְּנִימִי
לִהְיוֹת חִיצוֹן. רָמוּז כָּאן מְאֹרַע אַחֵר,
הִיא מְנַבֵּאת, אֲשֶׁר יִפְרֹץ, כְּמוֹ חַיָּה רָעָה,
מִסַּף-הַהַכָּרָה אֶל תּוֹךְ הַבַּיִת, וְיָמִיט אָסוֹן.

52

There are signs

There are signs at home, so my wife says,
signs of fingerprints, in the cracks in the house, on the floor tiles.
There is evidence of their presence.
And so I wonder to myself, how
can I make room for her, for her strange sensitivity,
signs that were, that will be and remain.

However, she insists, this matter is symbolic, universal, don't you see,
          like a dress,
she says, and demonstrates, turning her palm inside
out. They hint of a different struggle,
she prophesies, which will burst out like a wild animal
from the edge of consciousness into the house and cause disaster.

בחושך

גַּם בַּחֹשֶׁךְ הַדְּבָרִים זָזִים. יְשֵׁנָה
תְּנוּדָה סְמוּיָה בַּחֶדֶר. כּוֹס נִפְקַעַת
עַל הַשַּׁיִשׁ בַּמִּטְבָּח, וּבֶגֶד מִתְבַּלֶּה בְּשֶׁקֶט
עַל קוֹלָב. כְּלֵי הָאוֹיֵב, אִם מֻתָּר
לְהִתְבַּטֵּא כָּךְ, לְעוֹלָם אֵינָם נָחִים.

וְכָכָה, הַמָּקוֹם הַמְרֻחָק, הַמְיֻחָל כָּל-כָּךְ,
מִן הָאֵימָה הַזֹּאת, אֵימַת הַחֲפָצִים הַמְפֻרָרִים,
הַמִּתְמַלְּאִים פִּתְאֹם, בְּרַחַשׁ, בְּנוֹזֵל-טִינָה
שְׁקֵטָה כְּלַפֶּיךָ, הוּא בַּנְּפִילָה,
מִכָּאן, וּבְבַת-אַחַת, מְצוּק

הַתַּרְדֵּמָה הַחַד.

54

In the Dark Too

Things are on the move in the dark too, motion
hidden in the room. An abandoned cup
on the kitchen counter. A piece of clothing fading
quietly on a hanger. The enemy's weapons, if
one may speak this way, never rest.

And so, the longed for place, far from this threat,
the threat of objects that disintegrate
and fill suddenly, murmuring
with silent liquid spite for you,
is a fall
from here, all at once, from the sharp cliff

of a deep sleep.

לִקְרֹא שֵׁמוֹת

מִבַּעַד לְחַלּוֹן הַפְּלַסְטִיק הַשָּׁרוּט בַּתַּחֲנָה
הַמֶּרְכָּזִית רָאִיתִי זוּג צָעִיר. אָדָם
קַדְמוֹן וּלְיָדוֹ עָמְדָה אִשְׁתּוֹ
חַוָּה עַל-יַד הַקִּיר.
מִבַּעַד לְחַלּוֹן הַפְּלַסְטִיק הַשָּׁרוּט בַּגֶּשֶׁם
הָרִאשׁוֹן אֲשֶׁר זָלַג עַל הַחַלּוֹן בַּעֲנָוָה
רָאִיתִי זוּג צָעִיר. רָאִיתִי אֶת הָאִישׁ וְהוּא
הָיָה קָרוֹב-רָחוֹק שֶׁלִּי אִשְׁתּוֹ הָיְתָה גַּם הִיא
קְרוֹבָה. שֶׁלּוֹ מַקּוֹר עָדִין נָגַע קַלּוֹת
שֶׁלָּהּ בְּמַקּוֹרָהּ לָכֵן נָתַתִּי לוֹ לָאִישׁ
הַזֶּה שֵׁם שֶׁל צִפּוֹר טוֹבָה וּלְאִשְׁתּוֹ קָרָאתִי
צִפּוֹרָה.

Calling by Name

On the other side of the scratched plastic window
in the central bus station, I saw a young couple. Ancient Adam
and Eve his wife standing next to him by a wall.
On the other side of the scratched plastic window in the first
rain pounding humbly on the windows,
I saw a young couple. I saw the man,
a distant relative of mine and his wife
a relative too. His gentle beak lightly grazed
hers and so I named this
man Good Bird and his wife I called
Birdie.

מכתבים מאלוהים

א

הוּא כּוֹתֵב לִי בְּיָוָנִית תּוּרְכִּית אוֹ בּוּלְגָּרִית
סִדְרָה שֶׁל מִכְתָּבִים שׁוֹנִים עַל הָעוֹלָם הַזֶּה
זֶה אֱלֹהִים אַחֵר לְדַעְתִּי הַפַּעַם הוּא הַרְבֵּה
יוֹתֵר מַשְׂכִּיל פָּתוּחַ וְנָאוֹר

כָּךְ בְּפַשְׁטוּת עוֹלֶה לְדַעְתִּי מִתּוֹךְ
קְרִיאָה בְּמִכְתָּבִים הָאַחֲרוֹנִים שֶׁלּוֹ
עַתָּה הוּא מְפָרֵט הַרְבֵּה יוֹתֵר מִבְּעָבָר
מֵעֹז יוֹתֵר כּוֹתֵב דְּבָרִים גַּם עַל עַצְמוֹ

ב

בְּיָוָנִית קַלָּה תּוּרְכִּית אוֹ בּוּלְגָּרִית
לְעִתִּים הוּא גַּם מוֹנֶה וּמְפָרֵט לִי
רְשִׁימָה שֶׁל שְׁאֵלוֹת שׁוֹנוֹת
דְּבָרִים עַל הַתְּנוּעָה עַל הָאֶנֶרְגְּיָה

הוּא מַסְבִּיר כְּאִלּוּ לְתַמּוֹ
קְטָעִים מַהַלְכִים תְּמוּהִים
דְּבָרִים לֹא מוּבָנִים שֶׁנַּעֲשׂוּ לָאַחֲרוֹנָה

בְּיָוָנִית קַלָּה מְאֹד כְּדֵי שֶׁאָבִין
וּלְעִתִּים הוּא גַּם מַחֲלִיף
תּוּרְכִּית אוֹ בּוּלְגָּרִית

58

Letters from God

1.
He writes me a series of letters about this world
in Greek, Turkish or Bulgarian
it's a different God I think this time He's much
more learned, open and enlightened

so it simply occurs to me while reading
His recent letters
that now He gives more details than He used to
dares more to write about Himself

2.
in easy Greek, Turkish or Bulgarian
He often lists
various questions
about motion about energy

He explains puzzling changes
almost as if He didn't mean to,
incomprehensible things that have happened of late

in very easy Greek so I'll understand
and He often switches
into Turkish or Bulgarian

ג

אֲנִי סָבוּר שֶׁלֹּא אֶטְעֶה
אִם אֲנַסֶּה מַה שֶׁמִּשְׁתַּמֵּעַ
מֵרְמָזִים שׁוֹנִים בְּמִכְתָּבָיו
בְּאוֹפֶן זֶה

וַאֲנִי בֶּאֱמֶת רוֹצֶה
לִהְיוֹת זָהִיר

נִכָּר בּוֹ הָרָצוֹן
הַכֵּן לִהְיוֹת מוּבָן
לִהְיוֹת בָּהִיר
וּלְדַיֵּק בְּכָל מִלָּה

בְּתוֹר כּוֹתֵב
בּוֹדֵד שֶׁמְּדַמְיֵן לְבַד
אֶת סָבַךְ הָעֲלִילָה

ד

שֶׁל הָעוֹלָם
הַזֶּה בְּסַךְ הַכֹּל
אַתָּה מֵבִין

זְאֵב
זְאֵב בּוֹדֵד

60

3.
I think I won't go wrong
if I put into words this way
what arises from hints in His letters

I really want
to be careful here

His sincere desire
is to be understood
to be clear
and use every word precisely

as a writer on his own
imagining alone
the thickening plot

4.
of this
world after all
you understand

a wolf
a lone wolf

ה

זְאֵב בּוֹדֵד אֲבָל
בְּסוֹף מִכְתָּב אֶחָד
לַמְרוֹת אוֹתוֹ כְּאֵב

ו

לַמְרוֹת הַמָּוֶת
הָאוֹרֵב הוּא גַם
גֶּזֶר יָפֶה בְּמִסְפָּרַיִם

וְגַם הִדְבִּיק
חִיּוּךְ שֶׁלּוֹ

וּלְמַטָּה
בְּתַחְתִּית הַפֶּרַח
גַם צִיֵּר לִי לֵב

5.

the wolf runs away but
at the end of one letter
despite the pain

6.

despite death
lurking He also
cut nicely with scissors

and pasted
His smile

on the bottom
under the flower
and drew a heart for me

אַל תַּאֲשִׁימוּ אוֹתוֹ. הֵם נָהֲגוּ לִשְׁאֹל שְׁאֵלוֹת פּוֹגְעוֹת. הָיוּ לָהֶם
מַבָּטִים חוֹדְרִים. הַשִּׂיחוֹת הָאֲרֻכּוֹת אִתָּם הֵלְאוּ אוֹתוֹ בְּעוֹדוֹ צָעִיר
לְיָמִים. הֵם נָהֲגוּ לַחֲזֹר לְפָנָיו שׁוּב
וְשׁוּב עַל מִקְבְּצֵי הַמִּלִּים
חֲסְרוֹת־הַפֵּשֶׁר. הָיָה עָלָיו
לְהַקְדִּים שָׁלוֹם לְאַלְפֵי הַדְּמֻיּוֹת שֶׁהִגִּיחוּ אֵלָיו
מִמַּסְלוּל הַפֶּתַח הָרָחָב. הָיָה עָלָיו
לָקֹד מְנֻמָּס וְלִפְעֹר אֶת חִיּוּכוֹ הַמַּמְאִיר, אָסוּר
הָיָה לוֹ לְהִתְעַלֵּם מֵהַמַּעֲבָר הַמָּהִיר
שֶׁלָּהֶם לְמַצְּבֵי כְּרִיעָה. אָסוּר
הָיָה לוֹ לְהִתְעַלֵּם מִתִּקְתּוּק לְשׁוֹנָם
הַלֹּא־נִלְאָה, מְצֻוַּחַת
עוֹפוֹתֵיהֶם הַנִּשְׁחָטִים
מֵעַל שֻׁלְחֲנוֹת־הָעֵץ.
הִנֵּה מָלְאוּ לְךָ, בְּנֵנוּ הַיָּקָר, שְׁלֹשָׁה־
עָשָׂר אֲבִיבִים. חֲזַק וֶאֱמָץ. שָׂא בִּרְכוֹתֵינוּ הַלְּבָבִיּוֹת. שָׂא. שָׂא.
שָׂא.

אֲשָׁיוֹת הַחִנּוּךְ־הַמְּקוֹמִי הִתְמוֹטְטוּ
עַל הַיֶּלֶד הָרַךְ מִשֶּׁנִּגַּשׁ
לָשֵׂאת אֶת דְּבָרָיו לִפְנֵי הַקָּהָל
הָרַב. הַמִּיקְרוֹפוֹן הָלַךְ לְפָנָיו כְּמַטֶּטֶלֶת
וְרַעַד נוֹרָאוֹת מִשֶּׁנִּגַּשׁ הַיֶּלֶד הָרַךְ לָשֵׂאת דְּבָרִים לִפְנֵי
הַקָּהָל הָרַב.
אֶפְשָׁר שֶׁהָיוּ לוֹ כַּמָּה רַעְיוֹנוֹת יָפִים לוֹמַר,
בְּאוֹתוֹ עֶרֶב מַר, כְּשֶׁנֶּאֱלַם
לוֹ פִּיו הַקָּטָן, כְּשֶׁהֶחֱוִיר, הֶאֱדִים, וְשָׁעוּל
אַיֹּם תְּקָפוֹ וּפָרְחָה לוֹ
נַפְשׁוֹ הָעֲדִינָה.

64

Bar Mitzvah

Don't blame him. They asked hurtful questions. They had
piercing glances. Their long conversations wore the young boy
down. They repeated incomprehensible phrases again
and again. He had first
to greet the thousands of figures that jumped out at him
from an unguarded road. He had
to bow politely and broaden his malignant smile, forbidden
to ignore the speed with which they
crouched on bended knee. Forbidden
to ignore the unending rat-a-tat-tat
of their tongues, the screams
of their slaughtered chickens
above the wooden tables.
Now you have reached, our dear son, thirteen
springs. Be strong and brave. Bear our hearty blessings. Bear them. Bear them.
Bear them.

The foundations of the local educational system collapsed
around the tender boy when he stepped up to make his remarks to the large
crowd. The microphone as if shaken trembled terribly
when the boy approached to speak to the large crowd.
Perhaps he had a few good ideas to give them,
on that bitter evening, when his small mouth
was struck dumb, when he turned pale and then blushed,
and a terrible cough overtook him
and his gentle soul
flew.

ואם באנו לתאר

וְאִם בָּאנוּ
לְתָאֵר הַמְשׁוֹרֵר,
נֹאמַר כָּךְ:
אָדָם בַּעַל שָׂפָה רָפָה וּדְבָרִים
אֲחָדִים וְיָד מֻנַּחַת
עַל לֵב
נִרְעָד
כְּדָג לִפְנֵי הַפַּטִּישׁ.
(בַּלַּיִל,
כְּשֶׁהָעִיר חוֹזֶרֶת
וְנוֹחֶרֶת, הֲרֵי הוּא מֵעֵז
וּמַגְנִיב יָדוֹ מִבַּעַד לִלְבוּשׁוֹ,
הוּ אֵיזוֹ הַלַּמּוּת, יֹאמַר בְּאֶקְסְטָזָה.)
בַּיּוֹם,
פִּיו מַרְעִישׁ,
וּפָנָיו קָשׁוֹת
וּמְיֻבָּשׁוֹת.
קֶסֶם עֲבוֹדָתוֹ
בָּא לוֹ בַּלַּיִל,
וַתְּהִיָּה:
מִלִּים מֵעוֹלָם
לֹא רָאָה
נִקְבְּצוּ
בָּאוּ לוֹ, מִלִּים
שֶׁכָּאֵלּוּ, מֵעוֹלָם
הָאֱמֶת, לֹא
הֶעֱלָה עַל דַּל שְׂפָתָיו.
וּבְכֵן, הֲרֵי
פִּיו וְלִבּוֹ שָׁוִים וְדַרְכָּם
יִשְׁפֹּךְ הַדָּם. בְּקַדַּחְתָּנוּת
יִמְעֲדוּ
מִשְׁקְפָיו עַל אַפּוֹ

66

If we were

And if we were
to describe the poet,
put it this way:
a person with a weak tongue and few
words and a hand
resting on his heart
quivering
like a fish under the hammer.
(And at night,
when the city snores,
the poet dares to sneak a hand under his clothes,
such pounding he will say in ecstasy).
During the day
he growls,
his face rigid
and arid.
The magic of his trade
comes to him at night,
and the wonder:
words he'd never seen
gathered together like this
come to him, words like this
from the next
world that have not yet
risen to his thin lips, his paltry language.
Well, after all his mouth and heart
are equal,
blood pours through them.
In a fever
his glasses fall
down his nose

כְּשֶׁיֹּאמַר,
הַכִּשָּׁלוֹן, יֹאמַר
נָעוּץ בָּעֲבֹדָה שֶׁנָּתַן
אֶת עַצְמוֹ
כָּךְ לְהִדַּרְדֵּר,
וְלִרְעֹד
וּלְשׁוֹרֵר
וְלִרְעֹד
וּלְשׁוֹרֵר

when he mentions
failure,
and he will mention it,
attached to the fact that he let
himself
deteriorate so,
and quiver
and write
and quiver
and write.

איני מתנועע בשעת התפלה

אֵינֶנִּי מִתְנוֹעֵעַ בִּשְׁעַת הַתְּפִלָּה, אֲנִי עוֹמֵד קַר וְקָפוּא. דָּרוּךְ
לַבָּאוֹת. הַמַּחֲשָׁבוֹת מְטַפְּסוֹת עָלַי חֶרֶשׁ כְּמוֹ צְבָא-מְסַתַּנְּנִים,
נִתְפָּסוֹת לָהֶן זְרִיזוֹת בְּחַדֵּי-הָאֲבָנִים וּמַעְפִּילוֹת הָלְאָה.

אֵינֶנִּי מִתְנוֹעֵעַ בִּשְׁעַת הַתְּפִלָּה, אֲנִי עוֹמֵד קַר וְקָפוּא. בְּתוֹכִי זָרוּעַ זֶה
מִכְּבָר הַהֶרֶס, הַחֻרְבָּן. וְאִם אָמַרְתִּי כִּי אֵינֶנִּי מִתְנוֹעֵעַ
בִּשְׁעַת הַתְּפִלָּה, אַךְ בִּפְנִים הָאֲדָמָה הַקָּשָׁה כְּצוּר לִי נִבְקַעַת
בְּשֶׁבֶר וִילָלָה כְּלִסְעָרַת פֻּרְעָנוּת מְמַשְׁמֶשֶׁת.

אֵינֶנִּי מִתְנוֹעֵעַ בִּשְׁעַת הַתְּפִלָּה, אֲנִי מַשְׁלִיךְ אֶת צְרוֹר
מַפְתְּחוֹתַי אֶל-עַל וּמַעֲמִיד פְּנֵי מֵת. קַר וְקָפוּא.

70

I don't move during prayers

I don't move during prayers. I stand still, frozen. Ready
for what comes. Thoughts creep up on me like an army of infiltrators,
moving nimbly over the sharp stones, and climb onward.

I don't move during prayers. I stand still, frozen. Destruction and ruin
were planted in me a long time ago, and though I said that I don't move
during prayers, yet inside me the earth hard as a rock is rent
asunder and wails like an impending storm.

I don't move during prayers. I throw my bunch
of keys upward and pretend to be dead. Still and frozen.

ועם התפלה האני

וְעִם הַתְּפִלָּה
הָאֲנִי מְחַשֵּׁב לְהֵחָלֵץ כְּמוֹ פְּקָק. שֶׁעַם נִטְרָף
עַל מַיִם רַבִּים. אַדִּירִים.

לְהַתִּיךְ אֶת רִגְשַׁת הַנְּחִיתוּת. לְצָרְפָה לְהָפְכָהּ
לְשַׁרְשֶׁרֶת-כֶּסֶף-עֲדִינָה.

72

With Prayer, the Self

At prayer,
the self considers popping like a cork. A cork tossed
by many waters. Mighty ones.

To anneal feelings of inferiority, and solder, refine them
into a necklace of silver filigree.

אצלנו בחצר

לְאוֹר הַמּוּסָרִיּוּת הַיְרוּדָה שֶׁל הַיּוֹם יוֹרֵד
עַכְשָׁו הָעֶרֶב. לְאוֹר הַמּוּסָרִיּוּת הַקְּלוּשָׁה, לְאוֹר
הָאוֹר הָאַחֲרוֹן הַזֶּה שֶׁל הַתִּקְוָה, עִמּוֹ אֶפְשָׁר הָיָה
אוּלַי לָדוּן מְעַט עַל הַמָּאוֹר הַמִּתְחַסֵּר –
הִנֵּה הוּא בָּא, יוֹרֵד עַכְשָׁו, אֶצְלֵנוּ בֶּחָצֵר.

לְאוֹר פְּנֵיהֶם הַזְּעוּפוֹת, לְאוֹר הַסִּימָנִים
הַמְשֻׁחָתִים, כְּמוֹ צַלָּקוֹת עַל הַפָּנִים, לְאוֹר מַה
שֶּׁנּוֹתַר אֶצְלִי מִשְּׁאֵרִית הַיּוֹם, לְאוֹר כִּסּוּי הַפְּלַסְטִיק
הָאִים, שֶׁאֱלֹהִים אָרְגֵן בֵּינְתַיִם לָעוֹלָם הַמִּתְיַסֵּר –
הִנֵּה הוּא בָּא, יוֹרֵד עַכְשָׁו, אֶצְלֵנוּ בֶּחָצֵר.

לְאוֹר הַמַּשֶּׁהוּ הַדּוֹלֵף הַזֶּה בִּפְנִים,
לְאוֹר הַסַּכָּנָה הָאֲיֻמָּה, לְאוֹר
קִרְקוּר הַצְּפַרְדְּעִים הַמְצַרְצֵר,
הִנֵּה הוּא בָּא, יוֹרֵד עַכְשָׁו, אֶצְלֵנוּ בֶּחָצֵר.

יוֹרֵד, עַכְשָׁו, הָעֶרֶב, מְדַמְדֵּם, לְאַט,
וּמִשְׁתַּעֵל, כִּמְעֻשָּׁן כָּבֵד, וּמְדַבֵּר
עִבְרִית, בְּקוֹל נַחַר, עַל כָּךְ שֶׁאֲשַׁלֵּם,
שֶׁאֲשַׁלֵּם הַכֹּל, וּבְרַבִּית. לְפִי דְּבָרָיו,
הַלַּיְלָה בַּחֲצוֹת יָבוֹאוּ הַגּוֹבִים, עַל אוֹפַנּוֹעָיו
שֶׁל אֱלֹהִים. וּלְאוֹר כָּל זֶה,
בְּאוֹר הָרַע וְהַחוֹלֶה, בְּאוֹר הַמִּתְקַצֵּר –
הִנֵּה הוּא בָּא, יוֹרֵד עַכְשָׁו, אֶצְלֵנוּ בֶּחָצֵר.

In Our Backyard

In light of today's declining morality,
evening falls. In light of this slack morality, in light
of the last light of hope, with which we may
perhaps discuss the waning light —
here it comes, falling now, in our backyard.

In light of their angry faces, in light of the signs
of corruption, like facial scars, in light
of what is left for me of the remains of the day, in light of the awful
plastic covering God has arranged meanwhile for the suffering world —
here, it comes, falling now, in our backyard.

In light of something leaking inside,
in light of the terrible danger, in light
of the frogs croaking insistently,
here, it comes, falls now, in our backyard.

Falls, now, this evening, bleeds slowly
coughing like a heavy smoker, and speaks
Hebrew with a rough voice, saying *I'll pay,*
pay for everything, with interest. According to what he says,
the collectors will come at midnight, on the motorbikes
of God. In light of all this,
in the evil and sickly light, in the waning light —
here it comes, falling now, in our backyard.

אשת פוטיפר

לֹא יָשָׁר הָיָה הַשֶּׁקֶר, וְלֹא לְטַעְמִי.
מְשֹׁחָל בִּבְדִידוּתוֹ עַל צַד הַתֶּפֶר, רַךְ נִימוּס
וְגִנּוּנִים. מִדֵּי עָבְרוֹ אֲנִי שׁוֹאֶלֶת, מִנַּיִן לוֹ, לְזֶה
הַדֶּקֶר, קַו יָשָׁר כָּל כָּךְ וְהֶגְיוֹנִי. כָּךְ? לֹא
לִפְגֹּעַ לְעוֹלָם בַּדֶּלֶת? לְהָצִיץ לְצַד שֵׁנִי?

יָשָׁר? אֲנִי שׁוֹאֶלֶת,
הֲלֹא רָצִיתִי לְעַבֵּר
בְּאַהֲבָתִי בַּעֲבוּרוֹ אֶת כָּל הַבֶּגֶד, וְדַוְקָא
כָּכָה. בְּאוֹנִי. מְשַׁנִּים דַּרְכֵי הָעֶבֶד,
יוֹם נָתַתִּי בּוֹ מַבָּט, וּכְבָר הֶחֱוִיר, הָפַךְ
שָׂרוּל בִּגְדוֹ וְנָס, מַשְׁאִיר לַיָּד הַמְשׁוֹטֶטֶת
לִסְפֹּג לְבַד אֶת עֶלְבּוֹנִי.

לֹא יָשָׁר הָיָה הַשֶּׁקֶר. שָׁפָל
חֲסַר דִּמְיוֹן וְנִכְלוּלִי.
מִנְהַג הָעֶבֶד הָעִבְרִי הָיָה הַפַּעַם
חֵטְא חָמוּר לְטַעְמִי.
יוֹם לְיוֹם עָבְרָה רוּחוֹ אֶת הַמִּפְתָּן, מוֹדֶדֶת
בְּמַבָּט רָחוֹק וְקַר אֶת יְגוֹנִי.

אֲבָל רָאִיתִי גֶּדֶם. יָד רוֹעֶדֶת. כְּמֻשְׁתָּק.
וּבְעֶצֶם. לִרְצוֹנוֹ אוֹ לִרְצוֹנִי,
הֲלֹא מִמַּהוּתוֹ הָיָה יוֹסֵף כָּל כָּךְ פְּנִימִי, וְרוּחַ דַּק,
הָיָה עָלָיו לִנְהֹג אַחֶרֶת.

76

Potiphar's Wife

It wasn't an honest lie and it wasn't what I wanted.
Threaded in isolation along the seam, tenderly polite
and well-mannered. Now and then when he passes, I ask where did he get this
tool, such a straight and logical line. Like this? And he never
broke the door down? To see the other side?

Honest? I ask.
Didn't I want to impregnate the whole cloth
with my love for him
like this. With all my potency. Strange are the ways of a slave,
one day I gave him a look, and he turned pale, rolled
up his sleeves and disappeared, leaving behind my wandering hand
to absorb the insult alone.

It wasn't an honest lie. A creepy unimaginative
lie.
I thought that the way of the Hebrew slave
was a grave sin this time.
Every day his soul crossed the threshold, measuring
my sorrow with a cold and distant glance.

But I saw a stump. A hand trembling. As if paralyzed.
And whether it was my desire or his,
wasn't Joseph so introspective, his spirit so fine,
that objectively, he should have acted differently?

אַךְ הוּא פָּנָה פִּתְאֹם.
שִׁנָּה אֶת טַעְמוֹ,
סָטָה נִתַּק וְנָס. אַנָּס, צָעַקְתִּי
לְעֶבְרוֹ, אַנָּס, מָתַי תָּבוֹא?

וְכָל זַעֲקוֹתַי, קְרִיאוֹת הַשֶּׁבֶר,
רַק קָרְאוּ וּבָאוּ, מֵרָחוֹק
הִגִּיעוּ עֲבָדִים רַבִּים.

But he turned suddenly.
Changed his mind,
strayed, cut loose and left. Rapist, I shouted
at him, rapist, when will you show up?

And all my screams, the piercing cries,
just came and went,
and many slaves arrived from a distance.

תְּלִי אוֹתִי אֲהוּבָתִי בְּאַטְבֵי כְּבִיסָה.
וְכָל הַלַּיְלָה אֶתְנַדְנֵד. מוּל חַלּוֹנֵךְ. בַּחוּץ.

אָנָּא, תְּלִי אוֹתִי, זָרָה שֶׁלִּי – לְלֹא קִרְבָה – רוֹעֵד וּמִצְטַמְרֵר מִקֹּר.
תְּלִי קְרָסִים בְּחֶסְרוֹנִי. חַבְּרִי אוֹתָם – כְּמוֹ תְּשׁוּבָה – לַשֶּׁלֶד הַנָּעוּץ.

תְּלִי אוֹתִי בַּשְׁרִירוּתִי. וּבַמֻּפְלָא. בְּמַה שֶּׁאֵין לַחְקֹר.
תְּלִי אוֹתִי מִדַּעְתִּי, דְּלִילָה. מֵעַל הַחוּט שֶׁל הַמִּקְרֶה-הַמִּשְׁתַּלְשֵׁל.

תְּלִי אוֹתִי מִשְּׁתִיקָתִי. כִּשְׁאֵלָה.
תָּלוּי. חָבוּט. מָחוּץ.

הִנֵּה, רַק כָּךְ, בְּלֹא-מִלָּה,
וּכְשֶׁפִּי מֶשָׁל לוֹ חוּט-בַּרְזֶל –
אֹמַר לָךְ מַה נָחוּץ.

80

From the Songs of Samson

Hang me up with clothespins my love.
And I'll swing all night. Opposite your window. Outside.

Please hang me, my stranger — not a kinswoman — I'm trembling
    and shivering from the cold.
Hang clips into my absence. Attach them — like an answer — to
    the nailed skeleton.

Hang me by my free will. In wondrousness. In the unfathomable.
Hang me by my mind, Delilah. Above the string of arbitrary happenings.

Hang me by my silence. As a question.
Hanged. Bruised. Crushed.

Only this way, without a word
and with an iron thread strung in my mouth —
I'll tell you what's required.

למאיר

רָאִיתִי יוֹנָה מֻטֶּלֶת
לְלֹא רוּחַ חַיִּים.
אוּלַי הִיא מֵתָה בְּשֵׂיבָה טוֹבָה?
אֲבָל אִמָּא שֶׁלִּי רָבָה אִתִּי בַּבֹּקֶר מֻקְדָּם.

רָאִיתִי יוֹנָה מֻטֶּלֶת
לְלֹא רוּחַ חַיִּים.
אוּלַי הִיא מֵתָה בְּשֵׂיבָה טוֹבָה?
אֲבָל הָיָה בֵּין כְּנָפֶיהָ דָּם,
וְאִמָּא שֶׁלִּי צָעֲקָה עָלַי בַּבֹּקֶר מֻקְדָּם.

רָאִיתִי יוֹנָה מֻטֶּלֶת
לְלֹא רוּחַ חַיִּים.
אוּלַי הִיא מֵתָה בְּשֵׂיבָה טוֹבָה?
וְאוּלַי לֹא. מַקּוֹרָה הָיָה אֶל הָאַסְפַלְט
נָעוּץ. גּוּפִי רָעַד. יַלְקוּטִי הָיָה שָׁדוּף
וּמְצֻמָּק. וְהָיְתָה צִנָּה הָיָה שָׁרָב הָיְתָה רוּחַ
הָיָה מִדְבָּר הָיָה שֶׁלֶג הַכֹּל בְּיַחַד
עַל עוֹרִי הָיָה שֶׁצָּפַד וְחָמַר וְעָלָה
וְיָרַד כְּמוֹ סְפִינָה בּוֹעֶרֶת נַדְנֵדָה סְחַרְחֶרֶת
וַאֲיֻמָּה. אֲבָל הָיָה עַל צַוָּארָהּ וּבֵין כְּנָפֶיהָ דָּם.
וְאִמָּא שֶׁלִּי צָרְחָה בַּבֹּקֶר מֻקְדָּם. וְאָמְרָה
שֶׁלָּמָּה לָהּ לִחְיוֹת בִּכְלָל

I Saw a Dove

for Meir

I saw a dove
lifeless.
Perhaps she died of old age?
But my mother quarreled with me early in the morning.

I saw a dove sprawled
lifeless.
Perhaps she died of old age?
But there was blood on her wings,
and my mother shouted at me early in the morning.

I saw a dove sprawled
lifeless.
Perhaps she died of old age?
And perhaps not. Her beak pierced
the asphalt. My body shook, my schoolbag was barren
and shriveled. There was a chill a heat wave a wind
a desert and snow all together
drying and fermenting on my skin rising
and falling like a boat in flames a terrifying
merry-go-round. But there was blood on her neck and between her wings,
and my mother screamed in the early morning and said,
why should she live at all.

בגדי נסיך

בְּתוֹךְ הַמְּהוּמָה וְהַמִּגְגֶרֶת, הַחַיִּים
הַמְקֻמָּטִים, בְּתוֹךְ הָעִיר הַמְּעֻשֶּׁנֶת, לְפֶתַע,
בְּהֶסֵּחַ-הַדַּעַת, בְּמָבוֹי צְדָדִי, יְכַסֶּךָ יִשּׁוּב-הַדַּעַת
בְּבִגְדֵי-נָסִיךְ.

The Prince's Raiment

Inside the uproar, inside crumpled
life, inside the smoking city, suddenly,
without noticing, in an alleyway,
composure will clothe you
in a prince's raiment.

סמרטוטים רכים

קִיּוּם עָכוּר, רוֹפֵשׂ, עוֹד יוֹם מָאוּס, כְּמוֹ קוֹדְמוֹ,
גּוֹלֵשׁ, עַל חַלּוֹנִי, אָפֹר, לָעוּס, צָפוֹר-רֵיקוֹ מוּטַחַת
וּדְבוּקָה לַצַּד הַחִיצוֹנִי, וְאִישׁ לֹא מְנַקֶּה.

רַק הַנֶּפֶשׁ מִתְקוֹמֶמֶת,
כְּמוֹ חֲנִית מְשֻׁנֶּנָה נִזְקֶפֶת, אֶל הַלֹּא-
כְּלוּם בְּקַלּוֹנָהּ מוּטֶלֶת, כְּמוֹ
בַּרְזֶל עָקֹם. אַחַר-כָּךְ, מִשֶּׁנִּרְגְּעָה,
הִיא קָמָה וְעוֹטֶפֶת, כְּמוֹ זְכוּכִית דַּקָּה, לַהֲגִנָּה,
אֶת עֶלְבּוֹנָהּ, בִּסְמַרְטוּטִים רַכִּים.

Soft Rags

Murky existence, slops, another repulsive day like the one before
slides down my window, gray, chewed up, bird-spittle hurled
and stuck to the outside. No one bothers to clean.

Only the soul protests.
Like a thrusting spear, aimed toward no-
thing in infamy, like
a crooked iron bar. And afterwards, once it calms down,
it rises and wraps its pain, like fragile glass, for protection,
in soft rags.

מבוקש

מְבַקֵּשׁ מָקוֹם שָׁקֵט עָלָיו תּוּנַח הַנֶּפֶשׁ.
לְכַמָּה רְגָעִים בִּלְבַד.
מְבַקֵּשׁ מָקוֹם שֶׁיְּשַׁמֵּשׁ מִדְרָךְ לְכַף הָרֶגֶל.
לְכַמָּה רְגָעִים בִּלְבַד.

מְבַקֵּשׁ עָצִיץ, עָלֶה, גִּבְעוֹל, אוֹ שִׂיחַ, שֶׁלֹּא יָקוּם
וְיִתְקַפֵּל כְּשֶׁהִיא תָּבוֹא. לְכַמָּה רְגָעִים בִּלְבַד.

מְבַקֵּשׁ דִּבּוּר אֶחָד, נָקִי, נָעִים וְחַם שֶׁיְּשַׁמֵּשׁ סַפְסָל,
מִקְלָט, לְמִישֶׁהִי, קְרוֹבָה שֶׁלִּי, יַלְדָּה-יוֹנָה, נַפְשִׁי שֶׁלִּי,
אֲשֶׁר יָצְאָה מִן הַתֵּבָה, לְכַמָּה רְגָעִים, בִּשְׁעוֹת הַבֹּקֶר,
וְלֹא מָצְאָה מֵאָז מָנוֹחַ לְרַגְלָהּ.

מחנה צריפין, י"ז אייר תשמ"ט

Wanted

Wanted, a quiet place to rest the soul.
Just for a few moments.
Wanted, a place to rest the feet.
Just for a few moments.

Wanted, a plant, leaf, stalk or shrub, that won't
fold up when the soul arrives, just for a few moments.

Wanted, one phrase, clean, agreeable and warm to serve as a bench,
a refuge, for someone close to me, a dove-child, my own soul,
who left the ark this morning, for a few moments, in the early hours,
and couldn't find a place to rest her feet.

Tsriffin Army Base, 1989

אָמֵן, שֶׁתַּעֲשֶׂה אוֹתָנוּ קְטַנְטַנִּים כָּאֵלֶּה. קְטַנְטַנִּים
מְאֹד, בְּבַקָּשָׁה, מִתַּחַת לַגָּלַקְסְיוֹת הַגְּדוֹלוֹת שֶׁלְּךָ.
אָמֵן, שֶׁתַּעֲשֶׂה אוֹתָנוּ קְטַנְטַנִּים מְאֹד, בְּגֹדֶל זֶרֶת, מִתַּחַת
לַגָּלַקְסְיוֹת, לַשְּׁמָשׁוֹת, וְלַשְּׁבִילִים שֶׁל הֶחָלָב, הַמַּיִם, וְהָאוֹר הָעַז שֶׁלְּךָ.

אָמֵן, שֶׁתַּעֲשֶׂה אוֹתָנוּ בְּמִדָּה אַחֶרֶת, קְטַנְטַנִּים כָּאֵלֶּה, לֹא נִרְאִים, לֹא מְבִינִים
וְלֹא רוֹאִים בִּכְלָל מַה יֵּשׁ לְךָ מָה אֵין. מַה אִכְפַּת לְךָ? תַּעֲשֶׂה אוֹתָנוּ
פִּצְפּוֹנִים, בְּגֹדֶל זֶרֶת, וּנְהַלֶּלְךָ עַל כָּךְ, אָמֵן.

Hymn

Amen, make us into these tiny creatures. Very teeny
tiny ones, please, under your vast galaxies.
Amen, make us very tiny, pinky-size, under
the galaxies, suns, Milky Ways, waters and your blazing light.

Amen, make us a different size, tiny, invisible and uncomprehending,
unseeing of what you have or don't. What's it to you? Make us
itty-bitty, pinky-size, and we will praise you for it, amen.

אני מנסה בחושך לעורר אותך

אֲנִי מְנַסֶּה בַּחֹשֶׁךְ לְעוֹרֵר אוֹתְךָ.
מִמַּכָּה אוֹ מִירוּשָׁלַיִם.
אֲנִי מְנַסֶּה בַּחֹשֶׁךְ לְעוֹרֵר אוֹתְךָ.

אֲבָל אַתָּה יָשֵׁן לְבַד עַל אֲבָנִים קֵהוֹת.
וּמִי יוֹדֵעַ כַּמָּה זְמַן. בְּמַכָּה אוֹ
אוּלַי בִּירוּשָׁלַיִם, יֵשׁ
אוֹמְרִים מַמָּשׁ אַלְפַּיִם.
אוֹ הַרְבֵּה יוֹתֵר.

אֲבָל אֲנִי, עֲדַיִן, מְנַסֶּה, עִקֵּשׁ.
לֹא מְוַתֵּר. עֲדַיִן מְנַסֶּה
בְּכָל כֹּחִי, בַּחֹשֶׁךְ
לְעוֹרֵר אוֹתְךָ.

מִמַּכָּה אוֹ מְדִינָה.
יְרוּשָׁלַיִם אוֹ חֶבְרוֹן.

הַאִם בָּעֲלָטָה הַזֹּאת אַתָּה
שׁוֹמֵעַ אֶת קוֹלִי? יָמִינָה, שָׁם
לְמַטָּה, בַּנְּקֵבָה?

אַתָּה רוֹאֶה אוֹתִי?
נַעַר רַךְ, בְּאַפְלוּלִית
הַשִּׁגָּעוֹן?

כִּי כָּל הַלַּיְלָה מִיָּדָה
אֲנִי בְּךָ אֶת הַמִּלִּים,
וּמְצַפֶּה לְךָ,
לְלֹא סִבָּה.

מִמַּכָּה אוֹ מְדִינָה.
יְרוּשָׁלַיִם אוֹ חֶבְרוֹן.

I try to wake You in the dark

I try to wake You in the dark.
From Mecca or Jerusalem.
I try to wake You in the dark.

But You've been sleeping alone on dark stones.
Who knows for how long. In Mecca
or perhaps Jerusalem. Some say
millennia.
Or much longer.

But stubborn me, I still try.
I don't give up. I'm still trying,
giving it my all, in the dark,
to wake You up.

From Mecca or Medina.
Jerusalem or Hebron.

Can You hear my voice
in the dark? To the right, down
there, in the tunnel?

Can You see me?
A tender youth, in the dusk
of madness?

Because all through the night
I have been throwing words at You,
expecting You.
For no reason.

From Mecca or Medina.
Jerusalem or Hebron.

אוּלַי כַּמָּה מֵהֶם פָּגְעוּ בְּךְ?
תִּסְלַח לִי. הֲרֵי אֲנִי רַק מְנַסֶּה.
אוּלַי מָלְאוּ אַלְפַּיִם, אוֹ יוֹתֵר,
בַּחֹשֶׁךְ, לְעוֹרֵר.
בַּעֲדִינוּת רַבָּה.

עַכְשָׁו,
מִירוּשָׁלַיִם,

אוֹ
מִמֶּכָּה.

כִּי אִם תָּקוּם,

לְלֹא סִבָּה, וּבַחִיּוּךְ
אֲשֶׁר לִבִּי נִבָּא,
תֹּאמַר

פִּתְאֹם: "אַיֶּכָּה"??

94

Perhaps some of the words hurt You?
Forgive me. I am only trying.
Perhaps millennia or more have passed.
In the dark. To wake You up.
With great tenderness.

Now,
from Jerusalem,

or
from Mecca.

Because if You awaken,

spontaneously, with that smile,
as my heart predicted,
You will say

suddenly:
Where art thou?

יֵשׁ לִי דְּבוֹרִית בַּפֶּה.
גַּם לוֹ יֵשׁ דְּבוֹרִית. צְבָאִית.
כְּמוֹ שֶׁלִּי, אֲבָל פִּיָּה אַחֶרֶת.
אֲנַחְנוּ מְנַסִּים אֶת שַׂק הַשָּׂפָה.
אֶת הָעִבְרִית וְהָעֲרָבִית.
בְּמַכּוֹת שֶׁנָּאָה קְטַנּוֹת.
אֲנַחְנוּ מְנַסִּים אֶת שַׂק הַשָּׂפָה.
אֶת הַשַּׂק שֶׁל הָעִבְרִית,
וְאֶת הַשַּׂק שֶׁל הָעֲרָבִית.
בַּחֲבָטוֹת קְטַנּוֹת,
בִּכְדֵי לִרְאוֹת,
אִם רֹאשׁ הַדְּבוֹרִית
נִשְׁבָּר פִּתְאֹם לַחֲתִיכוֹת.
אֲנַחְנוּ מְטַלְטְלִים אֶת שַׂק הַשָּׂפָה.
עוֹשִׂים לוֹ נִסְיוֹנוֹת. כְּמוֹ עִנּוּיִים קְטַנִּים
לַחֲתוּלוֹת. וְלָמָּה? רַק
בִּכְדֵי לִרְאוֹת.
בְּכַמָּה בְּעִיטוֹת, בְּכַמָּה חֲבָטוֹת,
אוֹתָהּ שָׂפָה תּוּכַל סוֹף סוֹף לִלְמֹד?
עִם כַּמָּה חֲבָטוֹת תּוּכַל סוֹף סוֹף
אוֹתָהּ שָׂפָה לִחְיוֹת?
הַאִם זוֹ חֲתוּלָה עִבְרִית אוֹ עֲרָבִית?
לֹא מְשַׁנֶּה. אֲנַחְנוּ לוֹמְדִים עַכְשָׁו לִבְעֹט.
וּלְהַכּוֹת אוֹתָהּ חָזָק מְאֹד. בַּדְּבוֹרִית.
עוֹד כַּמָּה בְּעִיטוֹת הִיא יְכוֹלָה לִסְפֹּג?
אִם הִיא עֲרָבִית, אוֹ הִיא עִבְרִית.
לֹא מְשַׁנֶּה. אֲנַחְנוּ מְנַסִּים אוֹתָהּ בְּמִשְׂחָקִים.
בְּמִשְׂחָקִים שֶׁל נִסְיוֹנוֹת. בִּכְדֵי לִרְאוֹת.
כְּאִלּוּ הִיא פְּלָדָה, כְּאִלּוּ הִיא מַתֶּכֶת.
לֹא מְשַׁנֶּה. אֲנַחְנוּ גַּם יוֹרִים מְעַט בְּמִשְׂחָקִים.
כִּי לִי יֵשׁ דְּבוֹרִית, גַּם לוֹ
יֵשׁ דְּבוֹרִית, וְשְׁנֵינוּ מְשַׂחֲקִים.
לִשְׁנֵינוּ הַפִּיָּה שְׁבוּרָה עַכְשָׁו —

96

Games

I have a speaker phone in my mouth,
he also has one. A military model,
like mine, but with a different mouthpiece.
We are testing the language bag.
Hebrew and Arabic.
With hateful little smacks.
We are testing the language bag.
The Hebrew bag,
and the Arabic bag.
With small blows, in order to see
if the top of the mouthpiece
will suddenly break into bits.
We are shaking the language bag.
Making experiments on it. As if torturing cats
in moderation. And why? Just
in order to see.
How many knocks, how many blows
will it take that language to finally learn?
How many blows
can that language live with?
Is it a Hebrew or an Arabic cat?
It doesn't matter, we are learning to kick now.
To beat it very hard. With a speaker phone.
How many more blows can it stand?
Whether it's Arabic or Hebrew
doesn't matter. We are testing it with games.
Experimental games. In order to see.
Whether it is steel, or if it's plain metal.
It doesn't matter. We also shoot a bit during games.
Because I have a speaker phone, he has
one also, and the two of us play.
Both of our mouthpieces are broken now —

מֵהָעִבְרִית אוֹ הָעֲרָבִית.
בִּכְלָל לֹא מְשַׁנֶּה מַה מְּרַסְּקִים.
אוּלַי פִּיָה שׁוֹנָה,
אֲבָל שְׁבוּרָה לִרְסִיסִים.
אוּלַי פִּיָה דּוֹמָה,
אֲבָל שׁוֹנָה מְעַט,
פִּיָה בְּנוּיָה אַחֶרֶת.
פִּיָה עִבְרִית אוֹ עֲרָבִית. לְמִי זֶה
מְשַׁנֶּה בִּכְלָל מַה הִיא אוֹמֶרֶת,
וּלְאָן פּוֹנָה הַדְּבוּרִית.
הָעִקָּר, שֶׁהִיא
פִּיָה פּוֹחֶדֶת.
הִנֵּה, בְּשֹׁךְ הַמִּשְׂחָקִים,
נִפְתַּח אֶת כָּל הַמַּעְגָּלִים.
וְאָז, נוּכַל, כֻּלָּנוּ, בַּשַּׂקִּים,
כָּל הַקְּצִינִים, הַחַיָּלִים,
מִן הֶהָרִים לָרֶדֶת.

98

because of Hebrew or Arabic.
It doesn't matter at all what you break.
Perhaps it's a different mouthpiece
but broken to bits.
Perhaps it's a similar mouthpiece,
just a little different,
built a little differently.
A Hebrew or an Arabic mouthpiece. To whom
does it matter at all what it says,
and which direction it points.
The main thing is
the mouthpiece is afraid.
Here at the end of games,
we'll open all the circles up,
and then all of us,
the officers and the soldiers,
we'll descend the hills in bags.

יֵשׁ לָנוּ כּוֹחַ הַפְּשָׁטָה מַדְהִים

יֵשׁ לָנוּ כּוֹחַ הַפְּשָׁטָה מַדְהִים.
מַדְהִים. אֲנַחְנוּ רוֹאִים מִן
הַגִּבְעָה אֶת גּוּף הָרַע
הָעֲנָק גּוֹהֵר עַל הַשָּׁמַיִם
וּמַנְגִּישִׁים. אֲנַחְנוּ עוֹמְדִים
עַל גִּבְעָה גְּבוֹהָה וְרוֹאִים
בְּשִׁקְפוּת מַדְהִימָה אֶת גּוּף
הָרַע הָעֲנָק גּוֹהֵר עַל הַשָּׁמַיִם
וּמַנְגִּישִׁים. אֲנַחְנוּ עוֹמְדִים
עַל גִּבְעָה גְּבוֹהָה הַחוֹלֶשֶׁת
עַל בְּנֵי הַכְּפָרִים. אֲנַחְנוּ רוֹאִים מִכָּאן
הֵיטֵב כֵּיצַד גּוּף הָרַע הָעֲנָק הַנֵּקְד עוֹמֵד
וּמַזְרִים כּוֹחַ וְחֹם לִבְנֵי הָאֵלִים הַשְּׁרוּעִים
עַל מְטַת הַשָּׁמַיִם.

יֵשׁ לָנוּ כּוֹחַ הַפְּשָׁטָה מַדְהִים. מַדְהִים.
הִנֵּה, בַּתְּמוּנָה: בְּשִׁקְפוּת, בְּמִקּוּד, בְּבְהִירוּת
מַדְהִימָה: כֵּיצַד הָאֵלִים, וּבְאֵיזוֹ קוֹמָה, וְעַל אֵילוּ חוּטֵי
רְגָשׁוֹת אֲוִירִיִּים טְוּוּיִים, בְּעָרְמָה, תְּלוּיִים וְעוֹמְדִים
הַחַיִּים הָאֵלֶּה, עַכְבִישִׁיִּים, עֲצוּרֵי נְשִׁימָה,

מֵעַל מַעֲקֵה הַגְּבָהִים, הַמַּדְהִים
בְּיָפְיוֹ, שֶׁל גַּרְדּוֹם הָאֵימָה.

We have an amazing ability to make abstractions

We have an amazing ability to make abstractions.
Amazing. From the hill
we see the giant body
of evil lean over the sky
and breathe life into it. We stand
on a high hill and see
with amazing clarity the giant body of
evil lean over the sky
and breathe life into it. We stand
on a high hill overseeing
the people in the villages. From here
we see best how the giant spotted body of evil stands
raining power and heat on the children of the gods sprawled
on the bed of sky.

We have an amazing ability to make abstractions. Amazing.
Here in the picture: transparent, in focus and with amazing
clarity: how the gods and at what height, and on which
airy, woven threads of feeling, with cunning,
breathtakingly, this spidery life stands still and hangs

over the amazingly beautiful railing on high
over the gallows of horror.

פתק בכותל

אֲנַחְנוּ כָּכָה, בְּהִתְלַבְּטֻיּוֹת.
הַשֶּׁמֶשׁ לֹא רוֹצָה לִשְׁקֹעַ
וְהַשַּׁחַר לַעֲלוֹת. אֲנַחְנוּ
נַאֲמִין לְךָ בַּבֹּקֶר.

תִּרְאֶה, תִּרְאֶה בְּבַקָּשָׁה, זֶה
לֹא הֶסְכֵּם חָתוּם. בְּלֵית
בְּרֵרָה, אֲנַחְנוּ כָּכָה, זֶה, הַטֹּפֶס,

כָּל הַחֵלֶק שֶׁלְּמַעְלָה רֵיק. מָה אַתָּה רוֹצֶה?
הַכֹּל נוֹשֵׁר וּמִתְפָּרֵק. בַּחֵלֶק הָרָדוּם.
נוֹפֵל. כְּמוֹ שִׁנַּיִם רְקוּבוֹת. וְלֹא עָשִׂינוּ
כְּלוּם.

כִּמְעַט נָפַל לָנוּ לְמַטָּה, בַּדְּהִירָה
הַגּוּמִי, הַמַּחֲזִיק אֶת הַמּוֹשְׁכוֹת
הַחֲזָקוֹת שֶׁל הַגְּבוּרָה. נִשְׁאַרְנוּ כָּכָה.
בְּלִי תְּנוּעָה. כְּמוֹ פַּרְעֹה.
עַל הַסּוּסִים בְּתוֹךְ הַמַּיִם. נֵד.

לְלֹא בְּחִירָה. אֲבָל אַתָּה רָאִיתָ. סוֹף הַפֶּתֶק
עַד. הַפֶּתֶק הַמְקֻמָּט וְהֶעָלוּב.
הֲלֹא כָּתַבְתָּ בַּתּוֹרָה, מִן הַשָּׁמַיִם,
בַּלְּבָנָה עַל הַשְּׁחֹרָה. אַתָּה רָשַׁמְתָּ. בַּפְּסוּקִים
שֶׁלְּךָ כָּתוּב.

אֲבָל פִּתְאֹם בְּקַשְׁתְּ
מֵאָה חֲתִימוֹת! כְּאִלּוּ! מַה קָּרָה לְךָ?! זֶה לֹא מַסְפִּיק?!
תִּשְׁמַע, תִּשְׁמַע, בְּבֶהִילוּ, הָיוּ לְךָ בַּפֶּתֶק שֶׁבִּקֵּר כָּל הַבָּנִים,
כָּל הַשֵּׁמוֹת, יָכֹלְתָּ לְהָצִיץ!! אֲנַחְנוּ, כָּכָה, אֱלֹהִים, תִּשְׁמַע.
עֲזֹב אוֹתָנוּ רֶגַע מְמַלְאַךְ אֶחָד, מֵלִיץ! מֵאֵיפֹה לָנוּ? תִּשְׁמַע,

Note in the Western Wall

That's how we are, doubtful.
The sun doesn't want to set
nor the dawn to rise. We will believe in you
in the morning.

Look, please, it's
not a signed contract. There's no
alternative, that's how we are, the top part of the form

is blank. What do You want?
Everything is falling out, falling apart. Even the part that's sleeping
is falling. Like rotten teeth. And we haven't done
anything.

We almost dropped, while galloping,
the rubber band holding
the strong reins of courage.
That's where we're at.
Not moving. Like the Pharaoh.
On horses in the water. A wall of water.

No choice. But You saw. The bottom of the note
is witness. The crumpled, pathetic note.
Didn't You write it in the Torah, from heaven,
white on black. You wrote it down. It's written
in your verses.

But suddenly You asked
for a hundred signatures! As if we could! What's with You! Isn't this enough?!
Listen, listen, it's confusing, You had all the sons,
all the names, on the note in the wall. You could have peeked!! That's how we are,
    God, listen.
Lay off for a minute about that one angel, the intermediary. Where would we get

תִּשְׁמַע בְּבַקָּשָׁה אֶת זֶה, תִּשְׁמַע הֵיטֵב. עֲזֹב אוֹתָנוּ רֶגַע
מִזְכֻיּוֹת. אָבוֹת. מֵאֵיפֹה לָנוּ.

רֵד לְמַטָּה רֶגַע.
כִּמְעַט נָטוּי לָנוּ הַכֹּל,
בַּשְּׁאוֹל, הַצִּדָּה, אֵיזֶה עֹשֶׁר מַעֲלוֹת.
וְגַם הַקִּיר שֶׁלְּךָ, בְּהַרְעָשָׁה.
תַּחֲזִיק חָזָק. תִּשְׁמַע,
תִּשְׁמַע אוֹתִי, בְּבַקָּשָׁה.
הֲרֵי הַכֹּל הוֹלֵךְ לִפֹּל.

one, listen,
please listen to this, listen good. Lay off for a minute
about rights. Fathers. Where would we get them?

Come down here for a minute.
Almost everything is cockeyed
in hell, ten degrees off,
and your wall is being bombed.
Hold on tight. Listen,
listen to me please.
For everything is going to fall.

נַעֲשֶׂה אָדָם. מִמַּטְלִית מְשֻׁלֶּכֶת נַעֲשֶׂה אָדָם. מִשְּׁאֵרִיּוֹת
שֶׁל בַּד. נְבַלֵּל וּנְכַדֵּר, חָזָק, נִדְחֹס וְנַעֲשֶׂה לּוֹ פַּס
שָׂפָם יָפֶה וְחַד לְיָמִין, וּפַס יָפֶה וְחַד לִשְׂמֹאל, וּשְׁתֵּי יָדַיִם,
סְמַרְטוּטִים, נְגַלֵּל, יִהְיוּ לוֹ שְׁתֵּי עֵינַיִם כְּמוֹ תַּבְלוּל,
שֵׂעָר עַל מֵצַח-גַּל, כְּמוֹ סִירָה, וּלְחִי, מְגֻלְגָּל, חָלוּל,
וְאָז : סְטִירָה

עַזָּה וּמְצַלְצֶלֶת נַעֲנִיק לוֹ לָאָדָם הַזֶּה לַדֶּרֶךְ, שֶׁיָּקוּם,
שֶׁיִּתְקַיֵּם, שֶׁלֹּא יִבְהֶה. וְנַעֲשֶׂה לוֹ בֶּטֶן אֱנוֹשִׁית,
גְּדוֹלָה, שֶׁל כְּאֵבִים עַזִּים, שֶׁיִּתְפַּתֵּל, שֶׁלֹּא יַחֲלֹם,
מְעִי, קְרָבַיִם, שָׁפִין, מֵחֲלָקִים דְּחוּסִים שֶׁל צֶמֶר-גֶּפֶן,
שֶׁמֶן, מַיִם, מִיץ, וְנַעֲשֶׂה לוֹ אֵיבַר-מִין יָפֶה לְהוֹלָדָה,

הַמְּשֻׂכִיּוּת. וְדֹפֶן, רֶגֶל, מִצְלָעוֹת שֶׁל מִזְוָדָה,
וְנַעֲשֶׂה לּוֹ חוּט-שִׁדְרָה חָזָק וְאַפִּי. אִישִׁיּוּת. וַהֲבָנָה וְזִכָּרוֹן
עָמוּס וּמַתְּכִתִּי מֵחֲתִיכוֹת פַּחִים, וּמֹחַ מְפֻתָּל בְּשַׁקִּיּוֹת גְּדוֹלוֹת, מִכָּל מִינֵי פֵּרוֹת
מְמֻעָכִים. וְלֵב פּוֹעֵם, הוֹלֵם וְצַנּוֹרוֹת, כְּמוֹ חֲצוֹצְרוֹת-תְּרוּעָה, הַלֵּל לִכְלֵי
הַדָּם. נִקְרָא לְכָל הַמַּלְאָכִים : בְּיוֹם
שִׁשִּׁי בַּבֹּקֶר נַעֲשֶׂה
אָדָם.

An Invitation to the Angels

Let's create a man. We'll make a man from a castoff rag. From scraps
of cloth. We'll roll them into a ball, pack them down hard and draw a line,
a nice thin mustache on the right and one on the left and two hands,
rags, we will roll two eyes with cataracts,
hair waving over the forehead, like a boat, and a cheek, a round and hollow man,
and then: *Slap*

sharp and ringing, we will set this man on his way, so he'll stand up,
so he'll survive, so he won't daydream. And we will give him a human stomach,
large, with powerful aches, so he'll twist and turn, so he won't be dreamy,
a colon, guts, a point made of packed cotton wool,
oil, water, juice, and we will make him a beautiful sex organ for birth,

continuity. And a side and a foot, made from suitcase ribs,
and a strong spine we'll make for him, character. Personality. Understanding
          and a hazy
and metallic memory made of pieces of tin, the brain squirming in large sacks
          made of all kinds of
crushed fruit. A beating, pounding heart and tubes, like trumpets applauding,
          glorifying
blood vessels. We'll call all the angels: on Friday morning
we will make
a man.

האם את יכולה לחוש בפנים

הַאִם אַתְּ יְכוֹלָה לָחוּשׁ בִּפְנִים
מַה שֶּׁאֲנִי — בַּחֲלָקִים הַקְּטַנְטַנִּים
הַנֶּעֱרָמִים מֵעוֹלָמִי, עַל הַיָּה שֶׁבְּיָדֵךְ מִן
הָרִצְפָּה ?

הַאִם אַתְּ יְכוֹלָה לָחוּשׁ ? מָשָׁל, מָשָׁל... מָשָׁל
לְמָה בְּעֶצֶם ? אוּלַי מָשָׁל לְבַרְדְּלָס. מַה הוּא
מַרְגִּישׁ שְׁנִיָּה אַחַת לִפְנֵי שֶׁזְּנוּקוֹ
יְקֻפָּא ?

אוּלַי הַהִפָּתְחוּת הַבִּלְתִּי-רְצוֹנִית שֶׁל
הָאָזְנַיִם, הַנְּחִירַיִם, אוּלַי זֶה בַּתְּנוּעָה עַצְמָהּ, שֶׁל הַכִּוּוּץ
וְהַזִּקְפָה ?

אוּלַי הַמַּשֶּׁהוּ, הַפְּנִימִי, הָרַךְ, אֲשֶׁר עוֹבֵר עִם הָאֲוִיר הַחַם שֶׁבְּבִטְנָה,
בַּמִּטְבָּח, לִפְנֵי שֶׁיְּטַפְטֵף הַכֹּל — כָּל הָאֲנִי שֶׁלִּי נִשְׁפָּךְ —
לְתוֹךְ הַדְּלִי שֶׁלָּךְ, טִפָּהטִטָּפָה.

108

Can you feel inside

Can you feel inside
what I do — in the tiniest bits
from my world piling up, in the dustpan in your hand
on the floor?

Can you feel? An allegory, an allegory . . . an allegory
but about what? Perhaps about a cheetah . . . what does he
feel a second before his leap
freezes?

Perhaps the completely unwilled opening of
ears, nostrils, perhaps the movements themselves, contraction
and then erection?

Perhaps this something tender inside that moves in the hot savannah air,
in the kitchen, before everything drips out slowly — and all of my self spills —
into your bucket, dropbydrop.

אֲנִי כּוֹתֵב עַתָּה בְּסַ"ד פֵּרוּשׁ חָדָשׁ לַשָּׁדַיִם שֶׁלָּךְ.
חִבּוּר יָקָר וּמְבֹרָךְ, קִבַּצְתִּי בְּעָנְיִי מִפֵּרוּשִׁים שׁוֹנִים,
מִכָּל הַבָּא לַיָּד. מִדְרָשׁ נֶחְמָד, יַלְקוּט עוֹרֵךְ, עָדִין וָרַךְ,
בֵּין שְׁתֵּי שְׂפָתַי נִכְרָךְ.

עַל דֶּרֶךְ רֶמֶז, פְּשָׁט, וּדְרָשׁ וְסוֹד.
אֶכְתֹּב עַתָּה פֵּרוּשׁ נוֹעָז לְקַו הָאֶמְצַע.
פֵּרוּשׁ עַל נֶצַח, הוֹד, יְסוֹד.

פֵּרוּשׁ עָלִים, וְאוֹר בָּהִיר בֵּין עֲנָפִים,
בְּאוּר זוֹהַר עַל רֹאשׁ הָאִילָנוֹת.
וּבְדֶרֶךְ הַפַּרְדֵּס תָּבוֹאִי בּוֹ אִתִּי לָעִיר.
נֵלֵךְ, עִם כָּל הָאִמָּהוֹת.

אֲנִי הַדַּל כּוֹתֵב עַתָּה פֵּרוּשׁ חָדָשׁ לַדַּד בְּסַ"ד.
פֵּרוּשׁ חָדָשׁ וּמְחֻדָּשׁ מִמֶּנִּי עַל הַשַּׁד.
יַלְקוּט רוֹעִים קָטָן,
וְקוּנְטְרֵס נֶחְמָד.

הִנֵּה, קִבַּצְתִּי בְּעָנְיִי,
אֲנִי צָעִיר וָקֶט,
מִפֵּרוּשִׁים שׁוֹנִים שֶׁלִּי.
מִכָּל הַבָּא לַיָּד.

A New Commentary, with God's Help

I'm writing now, with God's help, a new commentary on your breasts,
a blessed composition. I have humbly gathered different interpretations
from everything at hand. A nice midrash, a tender anthology
bound between my two lips.

With hints, simple close readings, sermons and mysticism,
I'll now compose a daring interpretation of the Kabbalistic middle way.
A commentary on Eternity, Majesty, Foundation.

The meaning of leaves, bright light between the branches,
a radiant commentary on the treetops.
And through the grove you'll come with me to the city.
We'll go, with all the mothers.

Humble me, writing now with God's help a new commentary on the breast,
an innovative commentary of my own about the breast.
A pocket book,
a nice pamphlet.

Here, so young and inconsequential,
I humbly gather
my different interpretations,
from everything at hand.

סצֵינַת הָאַהֲבָה שֶׁלִּי צוּלְמָה מוּל הָעֵץ

סְצֵינַת הָאַהֲבָה שֶׁלִּי צֻלְּמָה מוּל הָעֵץ.
גֶּזַע וְצַמֶּרֶת רָעֲדוּ מֵהִתְרַגְּשׁוּת.
סַפְסָל נָסַע לְאַט נָסַק וְהִתְרוֹמֵם.
וְגַם שָׁמַיִם כְּחַלְחַלִּים עָבְרוּ אֵי שָׁם.

סְצֵינַת הָאַהֲבָה הָאַכְזָרִית שֶׁלִּי צֻלְּמָה
מוּל הָעֵץ. הָעֵץ בָּכָה מֵהִתְרַגְּשׁוּת. סַפְסָל
נָסַק וְהִתְרַסֵּק, פָּגַע בָּרָק, וְהַשָּׁמַיִם
הִתְקַדְּרוּ.

סְצֵינַת הָאַהֲבָה הַמַּדְהִימָה שֶׁלִּי צֻלְּמָה
מוּל הָעֵץ. הָעֵץ הָיָה חָשׂוּף עֵירֹם לְרֶגַע בַּבָּרָק
הָעַז. וְגַם אֲנִי. סַפְסָל נָע רַגְלַיִם נְבוֹכוֹת
בָּאֲדָמָה, גַּם הַשָּׁמַיִם נִרְתְּעוּ מִזֶּה, הִתְרַחֲקוּ
וְנִסְפְּגוּ הַרְחֵק בַּחֵיק הַחַם מֵעַל.

My Love Scene

My own love scene was shot in front of a tree.
The trunk and treetop shook with excitement.
A bench moved along slowly, took off and lifted up.
And blue skies passed over somewhere.

My cruel love scene was shot
in front of a tree. The tree cried out in excitement. A bench
took off and crashed, lightning struck, and the skies
darkened.

My astonishing love scene was shot
in front of a tree. The tree was exposed naked for a moment
by vigorous lightning. Me too. A bench dug its uneasy legs into
the ground, the skies flinched, grew farther away
and were absorbed by the distance, into the warm embrace above.

יותר ויותר צורדתו צורת גבר

יוֹתֵר וְיוֹתֵר צוּרָתוֹ צוּרַת גֶּבֶר.
וּפָחוֹת וּפָחוֹת מֵחָמְרֵי הָאִשָּׁה.

אִם תָּבוֹא מֵאָחוֹר:
לַעַ, שֶׁבֶר.
אִם תָּבוֹא מִלְּפָנִים
כְּמוֹ נִקְרָה רְגִישָׁה.

הָעֵינַיִם גַּמָּה,
הַשְּׂפָתַיִם פִּיר קֶבֶר,
רַךְּ,

כְּשֶׁהָעוֹר מְצוֹפָף
לְפָנִים בִּפְלִישָׁה.

הֶעָבָר, הֶעָתִיד,
מְקַבְּלִים
צוּרַת אֵבֶר,
נָח,

וּבָרְאִי
הַהֹוֶה
מִתְאַפֵּר
כְּאִשָּׁה.

More and more his form is that of a man

More and more his form is that of a man.
Less and less womanly substances.

If you approach from the back:
a mouth, a crack.
If from the front
it's like a sensitive grotto.

The eyes a dimple,
lips a tender hole
for a grave,

when skin gathers
forward during an incursion.

The past, the future
take on
the shape of an organ,
at rest,

and in the mirror,
the present time
puts on make-up
like a woman.

תפילה

אׇורת׳ודוקֶס מי נׇאוּ, מַיי דַרְלִינְג,
אׇורת׳ודוקֶס מי נׇאוּ, אֶרׇאוּנְד יוּ,
אׇורת׳ודוקֶס מי טַייט, מַיי דַרְלִינְג,
אׇורת׳ודוקֶס מי טַייטְלִי נׇאוּ.

אׇורת׳ודוקֶס מי, הוּ
מַיי לׇאב, גׇ׳רוּזׇלֶם !

אׇורת׳ודוקֶס מי טַייטְלִי נׇאוּ,
אׇורת׳ודוקֶס מי, סְטֶפ בַּיי סְטֶפ.
אׇורת׳ודוקֶס מי, רוֹף אֶרׇאוּנְד יוּ,
אׇורת׳ודוקֶס מי, אֶרׇאוּנְד יוֹר נֶק.

אׇורת׳ודוקֶס מי, יֶה ! הוּ
מַיי לׇאב גׇ׳רוּזׇלֶם ! הוּ
מַיי דַרְלִינְג ! אׇורת׳ודוקֶס מי
סְטרוֹנְג אֶנְד טַייטְלִי

אׇורת׳ודוקֶס מי פוֹרת׳ אֶנְד
בֶּק. אׇורת׳ודוקֶס מי, גׇ׳אסְט
אֶרׇאוּנְד יוּ. אׇורת׳ודוקֶס מי
רַייט אֶנְד הֶנְג. הוּ מַיי לׇאב,
גׇ׳רוּזׇלֶם ! אׇורת׳ודוקֶס מי !

הׇאבִּי לוֹאד אֶרׇאוּנְד מַיי נֶק.

A Prayer

Orthodox me now, my darling,
orthodox me now, around you,
orthodox me tight, my darling,
orthodox me tightly now.

Orthodox me, oh
my love, Jeruzalem!

Orthodox me tightly now,
orthodox me, step by step.
Orthodox me, rope around you,
orthodox me around your neck.

Orthodox me, yeah! Oh
my love Jeruzalem! Oh
my darling! Orthodox me
strong and tightly.

Orthodox me forth and
back. Orthodox me, just
around you. Orthodox me
right and hang. Oh my love,
Jeruzalem! Orthodox me!

Heavy load around my neck.

דֶלִיט מִי פְּלִיז,
דֶלִיט מִי אַבְּסוֹלוּטְלִי
פְרוֹם דֶ׳ה לִיסְט,

נוּ מוֹר יִזְרָאֶל, נוּ מוֹר
ג׳וּאִיש בְּלָאד, נוּ
מוֹר הִיסְטוֹרִי,

ג׳אסְט נָאתְׄינְג,
קְוַואִייט, פִיס,

דֶלִיט מִי, ג׳אסְט דֶלִיט,
אַיי בֶּג יוּ. פְּלִיז,

A Plea

Delete me please,
delete me absolutely
from da list,

no more Iz-rah-el, no more
Jewish blood, no
more history,

just no-ting,
quiet, peace,

delete me, just delete,
I beg you, please,

Notes to the Poems

What I Can

tfoo: denotes the tradition of spitting, or making a sound like spitting, in order to ward off the evil eye. According to Joshua Trachtenberg in his classic *Jewish Magic and Superstition* (1939), for Jews, "The most powerful liquid, as we have seen, was supposed to be spittle [. . .] Therefore it was suggested that one may protect himself [. . .] by spitting three times, and even evil thoughts, which are the work of demons, may be dispelled in the same way." http://www.sacred-texts.com/jud/jms/jms13.htm

Approaching You in English

tongue-tied, stammering: in Exodus 4:10, Moses tells God he is "slow of speech and of tongue;" *obscure speech:* Isaiah 33:19.

Lament for the Ninth of Av

The ninth day of the Jewish month of Av commemorates the destruction of the First and Second Temples in Jerusalem (in 586 B.C.E. and 70 C.E., respectively), and is traditionally observed by fasting, abstinence, and chanting the Book of Lamentations.

In those days there was no king: Judges 18:1, 21:25.

When the terrorists murder me at my window

Abraham's ram . . . Binding of Isaac: Genesis 22:1–19.

olive size for a blessing: The least amount (or size) for which a blessing must be said, according to Jewish law.

mezuzah: a parchment, usually placed in a decorative case, that contains specific verses from the Torah, and which is affixed to the doorposts of Jewish homes.

Verses to Be Added to the End of Deuteronomy

adversity and *contention:* Exodus 17:7: "And the name of the place was called Massah [a trial, adversity], and Meribah [contention], because of the striving of the children of Israel, and because they tried the Lord, saying: 'Is the Lord among us, or not?'"

A Poet

613 mitzvot: Refers to the 613 commandments in the Torah that are binding for religiously observant Jews.

If we were

a person with a weak tongue and few words: Genesis 11:1, "Now the whole earth had one language and few words."

I Don't Move During Prayers

is rent asunder: Isaiah 24:19.

Potiphar's Wife

Potiphar is the chief steward of Pharoah in the Joseph story in Genesis. His wife makes advances to Joseph in 39:7ff. and again in 39:12: "...she caught him [Joseph] by his garment, saying, 'Lie with me.' But he left his garment in her hand and fled."

I try to wake You in the dark

Where art thou?: Genesis 3:9.

Note in the Western Wall

In Jerusalem, the Western Wall is a remnant of a retaining wall of the Second Temple, the primary center of Jewish worship until it was destroyed in 70 C.E. by the conquering Romans. It is a site of pilgrimage and prayer, and visitors often leave notes with prayers or wishes in the cracks.

A wall of water: Exodus 14:20.

A New Commentary, with God's Help

midrash: a method of interpreting Jewish texts, often in the form of a short story or a retelling of a Biblical verse in order to explore its possible meanings.

Eternity, Majesty, Foundation: In Jewish mysticism, three of the "ten spheres of divine manifestation in which God emerges from His hidden abode" (Gershom Scholem, *Major Trends in Jewish Mysticism,* 3rd rev. ed. [New York: Schocken, 1961], p. 213.)

A Prayer and A Plea

"A Prayer" and "A Plea" are from a group of five poems written by Kosman using the Hebrew alphabet while the words are actually in English. Some English language sounds (for example, "th") do not exist in Hebrew.

Afterword: Gender and the Sanctity of the Jewish Home

By Shlomit Naim-Naor

KIDDUSH

I place obvious things down low on the table top.
I'm not misleading anyone, I'm not hiding anything, from this height, for me,
hovering doesn't add anything.
And so you can see the series of things where they were placed
on the white tablecloth, cup, fork, knife, and plate.

I make the blessing over the bread and cut a slice.
Also for you my wife. I make the blessing over the wine, sip
one-fourth. I exempt you in this way in my blessing, blessed is the one
    who brings forth
male and female into the world. And you, indeed, will drink this
liquid from my cup, and be done with your obligations.

Because your husband stands at a low stall and like a peddler counts the
    virtues of existence
and the praises of a reality which includes a series of things in place.
    Because suddenly this world arrives for him
on a white tablecloth, pure as a shroud, and in a cup and a fork and a
    knife and a plate.

In her book *Purity and Danger*, Mary Douglas points to the power of ritual, which supplies what she calls a "focusing mechanism" by setting aside a specific place and time, and arousing specific expectations. A "ritual provides a frame," Douglas writes. "The marked-off time or place alerts a special kind of expectancy, just as the oft-repeated 'Once upon a time' creates a mood receptive to fantastic tales."[1]

Admiel Kosman's poem "Kiddush" examines a ritual that is recited by observant Jews at least twice a week, on Friday evening and Saturday morning: the blessing over wine just prior to Sabbath meals. (It is also recited before meals on religious holidays.) The speaker in this poem questions the ceremony and the significance behind it, while deliberating on holiness in the home. In doing so, he examines the "tale" of gender told by the Kiddush ceremony as it is most often performed. He finds that the established practice of Kiddush reinforces a patriarchal assumption about the inferiority of women: the man (of the house) conducts the ceremony and the woman merely watches and confirms that it has taken place.

On a personal note: One Saturday I recited the blessing over the wine with my sister's family. My nephews, who study in Israel in what are known as national-religious schools (that is, schools for modern Orthodox Jews who support the state of Israel and serve in the army), were shocked. A woman may not perform this blessing, they thought. In response to a question I asked them, they responded that if there are no men in the vicinity, it is better not to recite the blessing at all — a stand which in fact contradicts Orthodox Jewish law, and which shows how the paternalistic approach clashes with religious law. According to the *Shulchan Aruch*,[2] Judaism's most authoritative legal code, women are obligated by the Torah to perform the Kiddush blessing "like men."[3]

In Kate Millett's *Sexual Politics,* she discusses Max Weber's claim that:

> "Domination in the quite general sense of power, i.e. the possibility of imposing one's will upon the behavior of other persons, can emerge in the most diverse forms." In this central passage of *Wirtschaft und Gesellschaft,* Weber is particularly interested in two such forms: control through social authority ("patriarchal, magisterial or princely") and control through economic force. In patriarchy as in other forms of domination "that control over economic goods, i.e. economic power is a frequent, often purposely, willed consequence of domination, as well as one of its most important instruments."[4]

Western society is fundamentally patriarchal, and the channels to power lie in men's hands. Even greater power is placed in the hands of men in the conservative sectors of observant Jewry, such as the one in which Kosman was raised.

In the poem "Kiddush," the speaker's dialectic approach to the entire ritual, and the distribution of gender roles in particular, is clear from the very first line of the poem. "I place obvious things down low on the table top." Just where is "down low" and where is the "top" and what are the "obvious things"? What makes something "low" or on "top" and in relation to what? These positions are unclear. And what is the role of such a sentence in a poem about Kiddush? After all, blessings and sanctity may apparently exist only in a world with distinct borders: holiness vs. impurity, what is permitted vs. what is forbidden — a world in which high and low are differentiated and men are differentiated from women.

After beginning with positive statements, the speaker makes several negative ones that testify to his reliability: "I'm not misleading any one, I'm not hiding anything, from this height, for me,/ hovering doesn't add anything." That is, the speaker claims he is telling the truth; and he says, "this height" — hovering, indicating distance from, or superiority over, women — doesn't do anything for him.

Why doesn't a superior position add anything? And, if this is true, why doesn't he do away with it? The following lines reveal a little about the world around him: "And so you can see the series of things where they were placed/ on the white tablecloth, cup, fork, knife, and plate." World order, and the system of coordinates which constructs it, revolve around ordinary items associated with women as caretakers of the household. However, while the dishes and silverware on the tablecloth are recalled, the house itself is not, and the table that contains them is also not mentioned here.

In the next stanza, the speaker continues to report on his deeds and relate to his wife. He describes the Kiddush ritual in detail, almost mechanically. This dry and precise description reveals the discriminatory point of view that he first adopts, and then exaggerates, ridicules and discredits.

I make the blessing over the bread and cut a slice.
Also for you my wife. I make the blessing over the wine, sip
one-fourth. I exempt you in this way in my blessing, blessed is the
         one who brings forth
male and female into the world. And you, indeed, will drink this
liquid from my cup, and be done with your obligations.

Is the blessing over the bread on behalf of his wife? What is the meaning of the expression "I exempt you in this way in my blessing"? Is it the meaning that many people often assume, that by carrying out the mitzvah he exempts his wife from having to carry it out? But then the woman is excluded from the concrete Jewish framework.

However, the blessing is also for "the one who brings forth/ male and female into the world." Perhaps the speaker's criticism is to be found here. The significance of Kiddush has become, not the sanctification of wine, but rather the sanctification of gender roles. The gratitude to God translates into an existential, gendered dichotomy between male and female. It also creates a divide between the realms of religion and existence, since the realm of the male is to exempt the female from religious obligation, and the place of the female is passive acceptance. She does not have to say anything aloud, or even to herself, but merely agree by taking a drink: "And you, indeed, will drink this/ liquid from my cup, and be done with your obligations."

Many women in Jewish sources are given something to drink by men, but Kosman usually favors more esoteric and surprising midrash[5] to well-known incidents in the Bible. In this case, the poem evokes the story of the *sotah*, the supposedly wayward wife, suspected of adultery. A test of drinking bitter water is enacted to bring the truth about her behavior to light. In the Babylonian Talmud, Tractate Sotah, Chapter 3, Part 4, the effect on a guilty woman is described this way: "She had scarcely finished drinking when her face turns green, her eyes protrude and her veins swell; and it is exclaimed, remove her that the temple-court be not defiled."[6]

In Sotah, the husband wields a great deal of power. Because of a mere suspicion that his wife has betrayed him, she must undergo a shockingly humiliating ceremony, in which she drinks a bitter brew which will provide proof of her wrongdoing on a sort of litmus paper that reveals the presence of adultery. There is no corresponding ceremony for men; men are allowed to conduct sexual relations with other women after marriage. Reading Kosman's "Kiddush" in this light, the line "drink this/ liquid from my cup, and be done with your obligations" nearly subverts the poem entirely, but its irony allows it to advance to the third and final stanza, in which the speaker mocks his actions: "Because your husband stands at a low stall and like a peddler counts the virtues of existence/ and the praises of a reality which includes a series of things in place. Because suddenly this world arrives for him/ on a white tablecloth, pure as a shroud, and in a cup and a fork and a knife and a plate."

We have returned to the similarly low surface we encountered at the beginning, but what is the husband doing now? He is not sanctifying, blessing or exempting; now he is located in a different awareness in which he counts unimportant things like a peddler. There is no point in praising reality or the virtues of existence. What is this reality made of anyway?

A tablecloth like a shroud, a cup, knife and plate. What is missing is the table top from the beginning of the poem. Now there is only a low stall, and the foundations of the house have suffered irreversible damage. The building of a home, metonymic for the shared life of a couple, is impossible if it is based on a gendered division of labor; no table remains standing in such a home.

In this poem, Kosman views the patriarchal allocation of gender roles in the classic observance of Judaism as the factor which prevents the establishment of a home as a complete whole. The white tablecloth of the Sabbath meal has become a shroud, and this division of roles, which prevents one of the partners from living a full life, expressive of its full potential, brings the image of death to mind: a spiritual rather than a physical death. If one cannot live fully in front of God or his-her partner, what is the essence of that life?

Endnotes

1. Mary Douglas, *Purity and Danger: An Analysis of Concepts of Pollution and Taboo, Collected Works, II* (London: Routledge Classics, 2002), p. 64.

2. The *Shulchan Aruch* (literally: Set Table), also known as the *Code of Jewish Law*, was authored in Safed, Palestine, by Yosef Karo in 1563 and published in Venice in 1565. Along with the commentaries about it, the *Shulchan Aruch* is the most widely accepted compilation of Jewish law ever written.

3. *Shulchan Aruch*, Orach Chaim Hilchot Shabbat 271:2.

4. Kate Millett, *Sexual Politics*, (New York: Doubleday, 1970), p. 45.

5. For a definition of midrash see the note to Kosman's poem "A New Commentary, with God's Help," in Notes to the Poems.

6. Babylonian Tractate, tr. Jews' College, London, ed. Rabbi Isidore Epstein, http://www.come-and-hear.com/talmud/index.html.

Admiel Kosman was born in Israel in 1957 to an observant Orthodox Jewish family. He was sent to Orthodox schools, then served in the army, studied at the Bezalel art college, and received a PhD in Talmud, the interpretation of Jewish law, ethics, customs and history. After teaching at Bar Ilan University for many years, Kosman moved to Berlin, where he is now professor of religious studies at Potsdam University and the academic director of the Abraham Geiger Reform Seminary, the first Reform rabbinical college in Germany to resume operations after the Holocaust. He has published nine books of poetry in Hebrew and three academic volumes of post-modern interpretations of midrash, one of which, *Men's World: Masculinity in Jewish Stories,* has been published in English by Ergon.

Lisa Katz is the co-editor of the Israeli pages of *Poetry International Web* and the translator of *Look There: New and Selected Poems of Agi Mishol* (Graywolf Press, 2006). Her book of poems, *Reconstruction,* was translated into Hebrew by Shahar Bram and published in 2009 (Am Oved). She works as a translator and book reviewer for the English edition of the daily *Haaretz* newspaper, and taught literary translation at Hebrew University from 2001 to 2010. She won the Mississippi Review Poetry Prize in 2008.

Shlomit Naim-Naor is the deputy director of Melitz, an educational organization in Jerusalem, and an international speaker on Israeli poetry, literature and Jewish texts. She holds an MA in Creative Writing from Ben Gurion University. She is a poet and a transalator and has written extensively about Kosman's poetry.